PHOTOGRAPH BY VICTOR KRAFT

AARON COPLAND

# Aaron Copland

---

ARTHUR BERGER

GREENWOOD PRESS, PUBLISHERS
WESTPORT, CONNECTICUT

The Library of Congress cataloged this book as follows:

**Berger, Arthur Victor,** 1912–
Aaron Copland [by] Arthur Berger. Westport, Conn., Greenwood Press [1971, ©1953]
vii, 120 p. illus. 23 cm.
Bibliography: p. 107–116.

1. Copland, Aaron, 1900–

ML410.C756B4 1971 785'.0924 [B] 79-136055
ISBN 0-8371-5205-4 MARC

Library of Congress 71 [4] MN





Originally published in 1953 by Oxford University Press, New York

Reprinted by permission of Oxford University Press, Inc.

Reprinted by Greenwood Press,
a division of Williamhouse-Regency Inc.

First Greenwood Reprinting 1971
Second Greenwood Reprinting 1975
Third Greenwood Reprinting 1976

Library of Congress Catalog Card Number 79-136055

ISBN 0-8371-5205-4

Printed in the United States of America

*TO MY WIFE*

NOTE

The musical examples in this book are reproduced by permission of the copyright owners:

Schoenberg's Suite for Piano, Op. 25, copyright 1925 by Universal Edition.

Stravinsky's *Octuor,* copyright 1924 by Edition Russe de Musique (Russischer Musikverlag) for all countries. Copyright assigned 1947 to Boosey & Hawkes, Inc., New York.

Copland's Piano Variations, copyright 1932; *Music for the Theater,* copyright 1932; First Symphony, copyright 1931; Piano Concerto, copyright 1929, all by Cos Cob Press (reissued under the auspices of Arrow Music Press, Inc.).

Copland's Two Pieces for Strings, copyright 1940 by Arrow Music Press, Inc.

Copland's Violin Sonata, copyright 1944; *Quiet City,* copyright 1941; *Statements,* copyright 1947; Piano Sonata, copyright 1942; *Danzón Cubano,* copyright 1943; *Lincoln Portrait,* copyright 1943; *Billy the Kid,* copyright 1941; *El Salón México,* copyright 1939; *Our Town,* copyright 1945; *Rodeo,* copyright 1945; Third Symphony, copyright 1947; Concerto for Clarinet, copyright 1950; *The Red Pony,* copyright 1951; *Twelve Poems of Emily Dickinson,* copyright 1951; Quartet for Piano and Strings, copyright 1952; *Sextet,* copyright 1952, all by Boosey & Hawkes, Inc.

# Preface

It is generally considered a virtue in a book on a creative personality to balance favorable comment against unfavorable. This is thought to make for an honest report, while anything approaching eulogy is suspiciously viewed as the expression of a fanatic or as a form of paid publicity. It should therefore be said at once that the effort spent in analyzing Aaron Copland's scores so closely would seem hardly worthwhile were it not for a conviction of their very high quality. The still greater effort to put these analyses into words would be pointless were it not a matter of primary concern to acquaint others with music that has aroused in me such strong feelings.

Reservations there are, though not many. And who can say that they represent anything beyond one observer's interpretation of the absolute values? More important and far more evident, I hope, in this book is the basic assumption that Copland's position among composers of our century is a lofty one. My aim has not been particularly to write a eulogy, because to some extent I tend to take his position for granted. But neither have I sought, in pursuit of what is generally regarded as a "fair" evaluation, to disguise the basic assumption, since this was what made me want to write a book about Copland in the first place.

The musically uninformed reader will have no trouble following Part One, since technical observations are reserved for later. But the reader interested in Copland mainly as a musician cannot afford to skim through these pages. For music is deeply involved in Copland's life—and not only his own music but musical activity in general. In this sense, he differs from the 19th-century Romantic whose life was deeply involved in his music, and whose loves and personal sorrows bear on specific musical passages, and thus must be recounted. Part One embraces, rather, the stages of Copland's musical evolution and his relation to the American musical scene as a whole. For these matters are inseparable from his profile, his travels, his concerns, his relation to his public.

The nucleus of this book was a Copland article I contributed to *The Musical Quarterly,* which has generously allowed me to draw on it; and *Tempo* has been similarly generous in allowing me to use excerpts from my articles on the folk aspects of his music and on his Third Symphony. To Nathan Broder I am indebted for providing the impetus to write this book and for his substantial editorial assistance. I also wish to thank Anthony Bruno and Donald Fuller for their helpful suggestions, R. D. Darrell for his collaboration on the discography, and Dorothy Markinko, Julia Smith, and Frani Muser for their aid on the bibliographical listings in the appendix. Copland's patience in offering his co-operation whenever it was sought was, needless to say, of incalculable value in the execution of this project.

*Arthur Berger*

*New York*
*May* 1, 1953

# Contents

*Part One*

# THE MAN

# I

## Early Musical Training

It has long ceased to be a norm for composers to appear on the scene as "descendants", in the terms of biographical jargon, "of a long line of illustrious musicians". The portrait of the young man clamoring for musical education, passionately seeking contact with serious musicians, struggling for sheer existence in a milieu consecrated to quite other things, is not uncommon nowadays, and to this class of individuals Aaron Copland belongs.

Copland's father left his native Russia at the age of fifteen, and after two years in England (where his Russian name, usually transliterated Kaplan, incidentally, was put down by the immigration officer as Copland) he settled in America and became a merchant—the owner of a fair-sized department store in Brooklyn. He was not even interested in music as a lay listener, and neither was his wife, also a native of Russia, who came here at the age of two.

Music of a sort was not, however, discouraged in the home. Even before radio had made its enforced and obsessive incursion upon the tranquillity of almost every American household, one could hear operatic potpourris and semi-popular favorites "passably", in Copland's own word, traversed by his older brother on the violin with his sister as accompanist, and there were also piles of ragtime on top of the upright piano for the "lighter" moments.

So Copland tells us in a charming and frank autobiographical chapter of his book, *Our New Music*,[1] and he adds that music in its more exalted manifestations "was the last thing anyone would have connected" either with his family or the "drab" Brooklyn street where he was born (November 14, 1900) and lived for twenty years. "Music as an art", he recalls, "is a discovery I made all by myself." When he was eight and a half years old his creative interests were foreshadowed in a song he wrote for his sister-in-law to show his gratitude after she had sent him cherries while he was sick with a mild case of typhoid. But in those years music was a matter of spontaneous play rather than methodic study with him. When he was eleven, he had abortive piano lessons from his older sister, Laurine. But these family arrangements rarely work out, and besides, Copland already had ideas of his own that led promptly to an impasse.

At thirteen he received his first formal piano lessons, and these soon brought in their wake more ambitious designs with regard to music. Copland's account of himself indicates the trials of these beginnings:

> The idea of becoming a composer seems gradually to have dawned upon me some time around 1916, when I was about fifteen years old. Before that I had taken the usual piano lessons, begun at my own insistence some two years previously. My parents were of the opinion that enough money had been invested in the musical training of the four older children with meager results and had no intention of squandering further funds on me. But despite the reasonableness of this argument, my persistence finally won them over. I distinctly remember with what fear and trembling I knocked on the door of Mr. Leopold Wolfsohn's piano studio on Clinton Avenue in Brooklyn, and—once again all by myself—arranged for piano lessons.

Thirteen is a fairly advanced age for a professional musician to start training, but his determination was such that things went rapidly. The fact that he began, after but

---

[1] In the following pages where Copland is quoted without credit given to the source, it is his autobiographical chapter, *Composer from Brooklyn*, in *Our New Music*, New York, 1941.

two years had passed, to consider the study of composition, indicates how strongly he was predisposed.

Copland was naive enough, when his interests turned towards composition, to think he could learn harmony through the proverbial correspondence course. But after a few trial lessons he knew better, and he got Wolfsohn to find him a theory teacher. In the fall of 1917, he began to study with Rubin Goldmark, nephew of the Karl Goldmark who was the composer of *The Queen of Sheba,* a rather celebrated work of that period. Goldmark, who was later to become head of the composition department of the Juilliard Graduate School of Music, was in those days teaching privately, and the aspiring young composer was thus deprived of the contact with other young people of similar aims that a school affords. His personal milieu could scarcely be expected to afford access to such circles. The extent to which he missed these associations is, I suspect, responsible to a degree for his efforts, later on, in bringing together budding composers and introducing them to one another and to vital contemporary musical trends.

Before long Copland inevitably found himself disturbed by Goldmark's conservatism. True, Copland, the mature composer, in looking back, now has respect for his first theory teacher's "excellent grasp of fundamentals" and ability to "impart his ideas", which were all a much needed fillip to a late start. As to his teacher's tendency to discourage "commerce with the 'moderns' ", even this had a productive effect as something to "whet any young man's appetite. The fact that the music was in some sense forbidden only increased its attractiveness." But this aspect of Goldmark's teaching was a limitation he would try to avoid in pursuing his subsequent studies. Meanwhile, he would uncover the new literature by himself. "Some instinct seemed to lead me logically", to revert again to Copland's own recollections, "from Chopin's waltzes to Haydn's sonatinas to Beethoven's sonatas to Wagner's operas. And from there it was but a step to Hugo Wolf's songs, to Debussy's preludes and to Scriabin's piano poems. In retrospect it all seems surprisingly orderly. As far as I can remember no one ever told me about 'modern music'. I apparently happened on it in the natural course of my musical explorations."

By his eighteenth birthday Copland was free to devote all his efforts to music, for in June 1918 he had graduated from Brooklyn Boys High School, and he had decided against pursuing his general education on a college level. It was around this time that traits of independence began to show themselves. *The Cat and the Mouse*, a piano piece written the following year, was already so advanced to Goldmark's ears (though we now look at it as a relatively mild effort of Copland) that teacher and pupil arrived at one of those untenable situations often marking the coming of age of vital creative talents. Goldmark admitted he had no standards by which to judge what he termed "modern experiments", and from now on Copland would have to do such things on his own, while at the same time preparing works for his lessons in a more conventional vein.

Under these conditions he continued with Goldmark through the spring of 1921, and to the piano piece he added another notable independent effort, *Old Poem* for voice and piano. *The Cat and the Mouse* and *Old Poem* would bear, in order, the opus numbers one and two if Copland had adopted this method of designating his music for they head chronologically the official list of the works he regards as professional in character—that is, beyond the stage of juvenilia or student endeavor.

During these years of study with Goldmark in composition, Copland assiduously applied himself to the piano as well, and he added Clarence Adler and Victor Wittgenstein to the list of his teachers in this field.

## Paris and Boulanger

In the summer of 1921 Copland went to Fontainebleau, where a music school for Americans was just being organized in the luxurious palace. The financing of this study trip abroad, which was in those days *de rigueur* for an ambitious musician of any type, was something he was able to accomplish partly by himself. Over a period of years he had saved money out of the allowances he had received from his father, who made a comfortable living from the department store. From time to time, too, the junior Copland would descend from his lofty esthetic sphere to help out as cashier in the store when there was a rush of business. He had also earned some money during the summers when he was sixteen and seventeen as a Wall Street runner, not because he was obliged to support himself, but because it was considered, in his circle, good experience for a young man. He had thus, all in all, accumulated a fairly sizable sum of money to help pay for the trip.

It is curiously symbolic that, in his eagerness to attend the proposed school at Fontainebleau, he should have been the first to enter his name on the enrollment list. For there he uncovered the potentialities of one of the faculty, Nadia Boulanger, as a teacher for American composers, and he was the first of a long line of creative musicians, among them some of the most accomplished, who came to study with her, encouraged by his glowing accounts of her pedagogy and by his later professional success.

It was unwittingly that he started this illustrious pilgrimage to her classes. He had come to Fontainebleau to study not with her but with Paul Vidal of the Paris Conservatoire, who, he soon found out, taught along the same conservative lines as Goldmark. Boulanger's course was in harmony, and though there were ecstatic reports of her manner of presentation, Copland took little notice of them, for he considered himself entirely above the level of instruction to which she was assigned. He was literally "dragged", it seems, to one of her sessions by a fellow student on the day she was analyzing a portion of *Boris Godounoff*. "I had never before", he tells us, "witnessed such enthusiasm and such clarity in teaching. I immediately suspected that I had found my teacher."

One thing made him hesitate. "No one to my knowledge had ever before thought of studying composition with a woman. The idea was absurd on the face of it. Everyone knows that the world has never produced a first-rate woman composer, so it follows that no woman could possibly hope to teach composition. Moreover, how would it sound to the folks back home?" Nevertheless, since his plan was to stay on in Paris through the year, it was to 36 rue Ballu, her home and studio, that he came in the fall.

"The influence of this remarkable woman on American creative music", Copland anticipates among his many eulogies, "will some day be written in full." Not all American musicians, however, have been at one with Copland as to the healthiness of this influence. It was said from time to time in the 'thirties that so strong an effect of a French musician must inevitably prove hostile to development of an American idiom. Nothing disputes this claim so much as the extraordinary way in which her Number-One-Pupil has evolved a style that presents complete contrast to the methods of previous generations of American composers precisely in its aspect of nationalism. From the vantage point of the present it thus seems odd indeed to look back upon the cavils directed on these grounds against what was contemptuously called the *"Boulangerie"* (the bakery)—the group that Boulanger encouraged by means of teas and class meetings (supplementing the private sessions) and that rallied quite understandably around her as around a venerated composer.

In this group spirit Copland found the musical companionship he had missed at home. Important to his development as composer, too, were the stimulating concerts he attended during that time. Copland has characterized the period as one in which "the pent-up energies of the war years were unloosed. Paris was an international proving ground for all the newest tendencies in music. Much of the music that had been written during the dark years of the war was now being heard for the first time." On his initial night in Paris, as a matter of fact, he stepped inadvertently into the midst of the excitement—a performance of Milhaud's *L'Homme et son désir,* with its sensational choreography that would be highly unlikely to get past an American board of censors, and Cocteau's *Les Mariées de la Tour Eiffel,* a work on which five members of the deliberately impudent "Six" collaborated. This was at the *Ballet Suédois,* to which he was directed by some impulse, rather than by the knowledge he would presently have that to go to this performance was "definitely the thing to do" among the intellectually élite that night.

He often returned to the ballet after that occasion, and there, as well as at *les Concerts Koussevitzky,* given at the Paris Opéra, he heard for the first time the provocative works of those composers who were then at the summit of their campaign to elevate novelty into a unique value. In addition to the music of the composers forming the "Six" (Milhaud, Poulenc, Honegger, Auric, Tailleferre, and Durey), he made the acquaintance of works of Stravinsky, Schoenberg, Bartók, Falla, Hindemith, Prokofieff, and others. Traditional laws were zealously being recast by all of them, and Copland, at his most impressionable stage, was fired with enthusiasm by this highly charged atmosphere.

Copland's stay in France, with the aid of additional funds from home, lengthened out from a projected year to three. In the course of that period he studied piano with Ricardo Viñes, Poulenc's teacher and a performer who may be credited with introducing many new works of French composers from Debussy down to Messiaen. Under Boulanger's guidance, Copland wrote four motets (a cappella), a Passacaglia for piano, a Rondino for string quartet, and *As it fell upon a day* for soprano, flute, and clarinet.

His most ambitious undertaking was a one-act ballet, *Grohg.* Not that there was a company to commission it—or even a choreographer. It was just that everyone was writing ballets at that time, and to do so became a "must" among the students. Under the enlightened dictatorship of Serge Diaghileff this genre was enjoying a powerful vogue. The

Russian impresario had provided the conditions under which music, among other arts, flourished and achieved astonishing vitality. It was difficult to conceive of new works in large forms as separate from his sensational ballet theater. A student who might normally, in another milieu, write a symphony as his first big work, was likely instead to write some accompanying score to a choreographic figment. Copland's imagination led him in a lugubrious direction. He had seen a German movie, *Nos Feratu,* along the lines of *The Cabinet of Dr. Caligari.* It was about a vampire who sucked blood from the necks of dead people. On this he based his *Grohg.*

Not until after Copland returned to America did the music see the light—and then in the concert hall, not in the theater. Part of the work, a short *Cortège Macabre,* entered the list of his orchestral pieces, and the better portions of the remainder of the ballet were later salvaged for his *Dance Symphony.*

In France he was introduced to audiences by more modest efforts. *The Cat and the Mouse* appeared on a school program at Fontainebleau in 1921, and Jacques Durand, who was in the audience, came up to Copland after the concert and offered to publish it. Copland was so deeply flattered at being approached by Debussy's publisher that he did not even pause to reflect when he was offered twenty-five dollars outright for the complete rights to the work. Referring to this incident, Hans Heinsheimer remarked to Copland years later: "It was the only business mistake you ever made."[1]

Copland's first experience in having music played at a public concert came soon after, in February 1922, under the auspices of the *Société Musicale Indépendente.* The work was the *Old Poem,* and it was performed through Boulanger's intervention. Its success was such that he was included on a program by this organization a year later.

---

[1] Hans W. Heinsheimer, *Aaron Copland,* in *Tomorrow,* Nov. 1947, pp. 6-14.

This time it was his Passacaglia, and the year after that *As it fell upon a day* was given.

## Repatriation

Before leaving France, Copland received a request from Boulanger to write a concerto for organ and orchestra. Her friend, Walter Damrosch, at that time conductor of the old New York Symphony, had invited her to come to America and appear as organ soloist with his orchestra in New York. In retrospect Copland is amazed at his courage in accepting, with little knowledge of the organ, with only one work in large form to his credit, and without ever having heard a note of his own orchestration. He arrived in America in June 1924, and shortly afterward went to Milford, Pa., to execute this commission under the singularly unconducive conditions of earning his board and living through the chore of playing piano in a hotel trio.

In the fall in New York, he completed the orchestration of his Symphony for Organ and Orchestra, which was the form his project of a concerto ultimately assumed. New York was just then responding to trends he had witnessed abroad, and he felt musically and intellectually quite at home. After the Parisian formula, *avant-garde* composer groups had formed the International Composers Guild of Edgar Varèse and the League of Composers. Marion Bauer, who has generously continued through the years to help gifted young creative musicians establish contact with the official world of music, brought him to the attention of the League, which invited him to play his *Cat and the Mouse* and Passacaglia in November. This was his introduction to the American public. A more imposing representation of his music came in January 1925, when the work written for Boulanger was conducted by Walter Damrosch in New York.

In those days the public at large regarded a modern composer as something of a naughty boy by whom it was both amused and shocked. This fascination accounted for the box-office appeal that no longer exists, now that the atmosphere of slapstick has happily disappeared. Around the time that Copland's symphony was given, for example, a thunder stick, employed in a performance of Henry Cowell's music at the International Composers Guild, accidentally flew across the hall and, according to the New York Times report, just missed critic and composer, "so that both lived to the end". The year before, Deems Taylor, then on the old New York World, had sent a sports reporter to another Cowell concert. Within the aura of such events, associated naively in the mind of the average concert-goer with physical violence, it was not surprising Damrosch turned to his audience, after Copland's symphony was applauded, and remarked: "If a young man at the age of twenty-three can write a symphony like that, in five years he will be ready to commit murder."

A second performance of the symphony took place soon afterwards, in February 1925, at a concert of the Boston Symphony Orchestra. This brought Copland into personal contact with Koussevitzky, who was in his first year as conductor of this organization, devoting himself fervently, as he had done in Paris, to promulgating new and vital music. A bond was immediately established, and the Russian-born conductor became the second of the two most decisive musical associations of his career. The other was, of course, Boulanger. Her role had been to energize the clear creative thinking, the sense of immaculate detail and formal logic that were innate in Copland. Koussevitzky's role, on the other hand, was in a more practical sphere. It was an advantage to be able to rely for so many years on an orchestra and a conductor of such distinction for the bestowal of initial benediction on each of his new orchestral works. In time, Copland's orchestral style began, reciprocally, to reflect the virtuosity of the Boston group. One may observe this effect on other composers too, whom Koussevitzky, so to speak, adopted. Some of these men, among them Roy Harris and younger composers like William Schuman or Leonard Bernstein, were brought to Koussevitzky's attention by Copland himself, who, inevitably first on this conductor's list, was never selfish in sharing his benefits with others he considered worthy of them.

Koussevitzky's characteristically Russian effusiveness over a new work that pleased him is all too familiar by now, and to take his pronouncements literally would provide us with an overwhelming and contradictory roster of "dee gree-atest" works. Such was the enthusiasm that fell at once upon Copland and his symphony, and he was promptly asked to compose a chamber-orchestra piece for a concert the League of Composers had invited Koussevitzky to conduct the following winter. Copland was too serious a young man to be spoiled by the conductor's lavish attention. He knew that his next work imposed a grave problem—to develop a more specifically American idiom after having absorbed so much of the European during his student days. To do so, moreover, without sacrificing the invaluable lessons he had learned from masters abroad. Jazz offered an obvious solution. Approaching it as a musician skilled in the traditions, he would have advantages over Gershwin, who had tried to fit his popular gifts into the frame of large forms he had not mastered.

Gershwin's intrusion into Carnegie Hall in 1925 had elicited cries of "sacrilege", and Copland too, with all his erudition and sophistication, was soon to encounter dissent for reasons other than his advanced harmonies alone. *Music for the Theater,* written for the League concert of November 1925, provoked the press[1] but was taken in the ordinary course of things by the "special" audience of modern-music lovers. A jazz concerto for piano for the general symphony public, a work unbridled not only in its cacophonies but in its "hot" polyphonies as well, was quite another matter. A veritable cabal was formed against this work in 1927 among staid Boston listeners, some of whom claimed that such music had no place in Symphony Hall and that Koussevitzky had given it with disguised

---

[1] See p. 23.

malice, namely, as a foreigner who wanted to show how bad American music is.

## Cycle of Departures and Returns

Copland's problem of reconciling his foreign gains to an American idiom was related to the broader one of repatriating himself after his glowing years abroad. He was quite different from the usual expatriate of that era, who was likely to return condescendingly to his native soil. He loved Paris, had profited from it as a musician, and had strong ambitions to go back. But he was also devoted to his home city, and wanted very much to express it in tones. When Boulanger visited New York in the mid-'twenties he proudly led her through her first tour of the Great White Way. Harold Clurman, one of his closest friends and to this day a faithful admirer, who had roomed with him in Paris, has recorded this incident in his book, *The Fervent Years.*[1] "It is *extra-ordinaire*", Boulanger observed, giving her characteristic, sprawling intonation to an epithet much used by her, "but not very *raffinated.*" And Clurman adds, "We didn't think of Broadway's lack of refinement. We thought it was *extra-ordinaire...*"

To understand how these allegiances to the here and there could repose side by side in Copland is to grasp one of the basic facets of his personality. It is part of his general capacity to reconcile opposites or shift gracefully between extremes—a capacity that has been acutely apprehended by Israel Citkowitz:

> One could no sooner describe a particular quality than its opposite would appear to counter it. In a less well-balanced personality these contradictions would create conflict and division. Copland can balance them, and, far from cancelling out, these opposites complement each other and work together like well-meshed gears. One could head his biography with the title, 'The Practical Poet', and that would indicate Copland's faculty of teaming opposites. A poet he is—any one of his scores,

---

[1] New York, 1945, p. 3.

whether intended for the concert stage, the movies, or a child's study period at the piano, displays his imaginative powers. And for his practicality, one need only plot a curve around some of the peripheral points in his career to recognize that only a person with an immense gift for practical organization could cover such a range without serious damage to his creative energies.[1]

Presently, we shall have opportunity to observe this success with the practicalities of existence. My purpose in pointing to this duality of spirit now is to anticipate those who might think it odd for Copland to love his city so much and constantly run away from it—or, what is more important, for a Brooklyn-born man of Russian-Jewish background to use, in the years to follow, Mexican tunes in *El Salón México* or Cuban formulas in *Danzón Cubano* as the records of travel impressions, or to found some of his major efforts on cowboy, New England, or Quaker folk music.

Those who know Copland, the man, realize that his passion for travel, his curiosity over what is going on abroad, is no greater than his yearning, before he has been away for very long, to get back to the American vortex of events. The various regional types of source material he has accumulated for musical substance, whether in his travels or from American archives, do not contradict the fact that through it all he remains singularly a New Yorker. And it is typical of the artist at work, as distinguished from one engaged in mere self-expression, that he is thus able to view his subject matter from without, realizing critically and astutely its implications.

To satisfy this craving to alternate periods at home with sojourns elsewhere he has mapped out his life with extraordinary shrewdness. He has managed so that fellowships for travel were at hand. And though he has, in New York and some nearby centers, done such things as teaching and lecturing for a livelihood, he has avoided regular jobs

---

[1] David Ewen, ed., *The Book of Modern Composers,* New York, 1942, p. 465.

that would tie him for any length of time to one place—or, for that matter, to one stagnating activity.

The problem of financial survival was not resolved immediately on his return from France, but a solution was not long in coming. Copland's first impulse was to establish himself as a teacher, and he forthwith opened a studio in Manhattan and dispatched printed announcements. These efforts brought him not a single response. Salvation was to come from a very different direction. His return from Paris in 1924 to embark on a professional career as composer coincided with the pre-depression years when benefactors for artists were plentiful, and he soon found himself in a position where it became no longer necessary to resort to jobs like the one at Milford. The events leading up to his good fortune date back to the League of Composers concert in November of that year. Paul Rosenfeld had been there and had been so deeply moved that he called Copland on the telephone the next day and congratulated him very warmly. The young composer considered this no less a surprise than "if President Coolidge had telephoned". While an adolescent, he had, as alert adolescents continued to do for many years to follow, discovered in Rosenfeld's ecstatic prose a kind of wonderland, where names unmentioned or unrespected elsewhere seemed to open up an entirely new, and the only valid, world of art. The ivory-towered concern with the most esoteric, the least commercial, phases of new creative effort was not of a kind to lead one to expect practical solutions from Rosenfeld. But his passion to support vital new trends carried, in more than just Copland's case, beyond the stage of self-glorifying prose. The appeal for a patron was conveyed to the critic through a mutual friend, Minna Lederman, editor of *Modern Music,* and Rosenfeld promptly produced one, Alma Morgenthau, to whom lovers of art are profoundly indebted for her altruistic assistance both to creative individuals and to projects like the Cos Cob Press, which she financed.[1]

---

[1] The Cos Cob Press was started in February 1929, at a time when the established, commercial firms printed far fewer of the better American

Copland did not require support for long, since it was around that time that the Guggenheim Memorial Foundation was established and he was chosen as the composer to receive subsidy during its first year, 1925-26. The fellowship was renewed for the year 1926-27. With the aid of the Guggenheim funds he spent part of each fellowship year (spring and summer) in Europe, staying this time not only in France, but in Germany as well. Among his musical companions abroad was Roy Harris, whom he had met at the MacDowell Colony in the summer of 1925. Copland had been much impressed by the natural impact and force of Harris's inspirations, and had persuaded him to study with Boulanger as a step towards acquiring the technique for their proper embodiment.

In later years Copland was to enlarge the field of his travels by adding to the European terrain the Latin American countries. In the early 'thirties Mexico, where his close friend Carlos Chávez has long occupied a key position in musical circles, became as favored a visiting ground for him as Paris. When World War II started, moreover, Mexican travel was understandably more feasible than travel to Europe, and this direction subsequently widened itself to include several Latin American countries. The new political policies of the United States, embracing good neighborly relations, moreover, brought in their wake endowments for travel in those parts. The office of the Co-ordinator of Inter-American Relations, in 1941, subsidized a good-will tour, with specific cultural objectives, and enabled him to visit nine Latin American countries. In 1947

---

works than they do now. The aim was to publish music of quality, rather than works that would bring large profits. The altruistic venture later merged with the Arrow Music Press. The basis is still the same. A committee of composers runs it, and selects the works to be published, maintaining a high standard that has given the catalogue prestige despite the fact that it remains a small and restricted one. The composer receives half of the receipts from his works, rather than the usual smaller percentage. The success of Louis Gruenberg's *Emperor Jones* in 1932 helped bring the Cos Cob catalogue recognition. For years it was the major publishing outlet for such distinguished composers as Copland, Virgil Thomson, Walter Piston, and many others, until the big firms took them over.

the State Department subsidized another excursion, confined this time to three countries.

Even within the United States Copland tends to move about. There were the years when he would flee New York periodically for the refreshing atmosphere and extraordinary working conditions of Yaddo or the MacDowell Colony. Then there has been Hollywood to claim him from time to time—for *Of Mice and Men* in 1939, *Our Town* in 1940, *North Star* in 1943, and *The Red Pony* and *The Heiress* in 1948. The invitation to compose for Hollywood was extended to him as a result of his success with the score for a relatively modest movie project, the documentary, *The City,* first shown at the New York World's Fair in 1939. For several years his work for the big commercial movie companies accounted for a major part of his income. We shall have occasion later to observe the remarkable degree to which he avoided descending to the level of the usual Hollywood scores, and how he exerted an influence on some of the resident, routine composers there and helped raise the general standards. He remained a composer of prestige who was brought in from the outside. Apart from the understandable fascination of the medium itself, there has been the important consideration that in the space of several weeks he has been able to earn, for one film, enough to carry him through his independent musical projects.

Another source of income for Copland has been his sporadic teaching and lecturing activity that dates back to 1927, and here once again Rosenfeld was the intermediary. Rosenfeld decided against continuing a course in contemporary music at the New School for Social Research, and turned it over to the young composer, who lectured there on and off until 1937. These intermittent lectures, and some teaching at the Henry Street Settlement, were supplemented by a term at Harvard University in 1935, at which time Copland replaced Walter Piston, who was on leave. He again replaced Piston in 1944, and for the academic year of 1951-'52 he returned to Harvard as the Charles Eliot

Norton Lecturer, a post in which he had such distinguished composer predecessors as Stravinsky and Hindemith.

But the appeal of an academic setting, or for that matter, of any pursuit, would no doubt dwindle very rapidly for Copland if he were subjected for any length of time to a routine. The closest he has come, therefore, to a commitment involving a recurrent pattern year after year has been as a member of the Berkshire Music Center, where he has taught since its establishment in 1940 and where he strives to foster the late Koussevitzky's ideal. But this has necessitated no great sacrifice of personal freedom, requiring, as it does, only six weeks each summer. Even this degree of regularity in Copland's life is, however, surprising indeed, and may be accounted for only by the very powerful coincidence of his allegiance to Koussevitzky, founder of the Center, and the opportunity granted for a limited indulgence of a genuine love to impart, as teacher, judgments that have been described by his students as extraordinarily impartial and perceptive.

## Extracurricular Activities

Copland's travels have always seemed remarkably unconditioned by the usual vague, romantic restlessness of the artist. Associated with them has been a sober need for constant self-renewal rather than a need for escape. If there has been anything for him to escape it has been nothing more serious than the intrusions on his time becoming more and more obsessive as he has involved himself more and more in New York's musical life—an involvement that seems especially remarkable for one who pursues so faithfully the straight line of a composing career. The versatility that has qualified him for the successful discharge of duties as a teacher has also made him much in demand in other spheres, and this demand has naturally increased in proportion to the growing fame of his music. Among the activities he has been known to undertake with address are those of lecturer, writer on musical subjects, a moderator of forums, and an organizer of contemporary-composer groups. His writings have included three books, *What to Listen for in Music*, *Our New Music*, and *Music and Imagination,* and contributions to such magazines as *The New Republic*, *The Musical Quarterly*, *The American Mercury*, and *The American Scholar* (see appendix). His critical articles were among the mainstays of *Modern Music,* until that invaluable magazine ceased publication at considerable loss to the music world.

Copland's organizational pursuits have centered around the League of Composers, where he has been for some time the prime moving figure in matters of artistic policy. But his efforts on behalf of vital new music—American music in particular—have been exerted in several other directions as well. With Roger Sessions, he presented the Copland-Sessions Concerts in New York from 1928 to 1931. In 1932 he originated summer festivals at Yaddo, Saratoga Springs. In 1937, he helped found the American Composers Alliance, a fee-collecting society for composers who do not operate on the grander, more remunerative scale of members of the American Society of Composers, Authors and Publishers. Copland was president of ACA until 1945, but his own increased success ultimately made it logical for him to join ASCAP.

He has also been active on the boards of such benefactory organizations as the Koussevitzky Music Foundation, the MacDowell Association, the Composers Forum, and the Naumburg Foundation, and he has taken part, from its inception, in the cooperative music publishing venture, Cos Cob Press (later Arrow Music Press).

In the early 'thirties Copland gathered around him several gifted young composers and encouraged them to form the Young Composers Group. This was modeled after the French "Six", who had found it easier to get a hearing for their works by functioning as a unit and with the aid of a definite platform propagandized by the critic, Paul Collaer, and the poet, Jean Cocteau. The Young Composers Group was introduced to the public at a New School concert, Jan. 15, 1933. Its members were Paul Bowles, Henry Brant, Israel Citkowitz, Lehman Engel, Vivian Fine, Irwin Heilner, Bernard Herrmann, Jerome Moross, and Elie Siegmeister. My own first contact with Copland came when I was invited to become part of this circle of composers. Since I was also a critic I could perform the function that Collaer had performed for the "Six". My article on the group, following the precedent of the French campaign, appeared shortly after the concert.[1]

Copland's organizing activity, while motivated primarily by a desire to improve the lot of the generally neglected contemporary composer through united action, received further impetus from his sociability as an individual. The usual display of ego, the genius-complex of the artist, inherited from the 19th century, is completely absent from Copland's manner and dealings with people. He has, further, an equanimity that serves to counteract the clash of egos among those with whom he associates. "Amid the after-concert gatherings that Copland relishes", Citkowitz has observed, "he sits with an air of serene impartiality that makes everyone else seem like a youthful barbarian. Yet with this goes an ingenuousness and wit almost childlike in their effect—just as a child's detachment from the turmoil and preoccupations of its elders can point up their foibles with devastating clarity."[2] It was thus that Copland was a stabilizing influence for the jealousies and inevitable violent dissensions of budding young talents. At times the sessions of the Young Composers Group became so stormy that even his powers of assuagement were taxed, and on one occasion a card inviting us to a meeting warned us succinctly, "no polemics". But when Copland was away, complete disunity was likely to set in among its ranks.

## The Days of the Select Audiences

The period of Copland's most intense devotion to the

---

[1] In *Trend,* Vol. II, No. 3.

[2] Citkowitz, *op. cit.,* p. 466.

ideal of the coterie and the modern-music society is paralleled by certain developments in his music. The validity of an art of a more intense, one might say specialized, kind has long been established. It is reflected in many revered masterpieces, from Bach's *Art of the Fugue* and Rabelais's *Gargantua* down to Schoenberg's Serenade, Op. 24, and Joyce's *Finnegans Wake*. Around 1930, whole groups among the intellectuals were devoted to this ideal of the "chosen". Outsiders branded such groups with the label of "snobbism". But lacking support of numbers and the big commercial enterprises, how else could these intellectuals and their small following establish a sense of the importance of what they were doing artistically? Perhaps there was connected with these enterprises some snobbism that was not the most desirable thing in the world, but one may condone and even welcome it when used as a defense against the destructive influences of vested interests.

The more specialized and esoteric works of art, which first have a limited audience, often become more comprehensible to larger and larger audiences as time goes by and there is more opportunity to apprehend their content, or after those who have understood them earlier have applied themselves to the task of elucidating them to the others. And sometimes works that seem incomprehensible at first communicate themselves so easily later that it is hard to believe they were ever difficult to grasp. It is not always easy to distinguish between those difficulties created by the subtlety and intricacy of the intrinsic relations and those created by elements of novelty, such as dissonance and unusual rhythm. Both types of difficulty are often present in great works of art, and it is obvious that any organized group dedicated to their defense, against a general public that is unwilling to take the necessary pains they impose, will end up by encouraging precisely these aspects of creative endeavor.

It was to this tendency that Copland responded around 1930 and he produced, under its influence, some masterpieces that will undoubtedly endure. Demotic elements of jazz are relinquished, or at least not overtly expressed, and the feeling content becomes more rarefied. The transition is already observed in 1929 in the *Symphonic Ode,* which, Copland believes, brings to a close the first major period of his evolution. That work marked the beginning of a noticeable change in his relations with public and press. Previously, of course, there had been no absence of dissension over his music. Mention has already been made of the war over his jazz-inspired music and its claim to receive serious attention. But quite apart from this consideration there had been the matter of dissonance to ruffle the conservative wing. W. J. Henderson of the New York Sun, reviewing *Music for the Theater* on Jan. 8, 1926, summed up the attitude of this particular wing with the general observation that his "music betrays as a whole a great anxiety to be modernistic while the modernist lamp holds out to burn".

The use of jazz in the Piano Concerto was not quite the means of easy access to the public that it had been in *Music for the Theater.* For Copland's sources more than ever were the most unbridled methods of free jazz improvisation which even today are looked upon dubiously and suspiciously by the majority of the public for whom the "sweet", commercial popular music represents the only acceptable type of "jazz". H. T. Parker of the Boston Transcript, Copland's staunch defender against the violent attacks from Boston symphony-goers, made it very clear in the columns of his newspaper on February 5, 1927, how advanced this jazz, served up by Copland with the latest European stridencies of harmony, appeared even in his eyes. Copland, he observed, "speaks for a 'chapel' of young American composers, for a new and experimental sort of American music".

When the Concerto reached New York, Lawrence Gilman of the New York Herald Tribune came promptly to Copland's defence in his characteristically eloquent prose. He found the work, as we may gather from his review of February 4, 1927, to possess the "fullness and authenticity of life which makes it at once perturbing and richly treasurable". Here was a work conceived "knowingly, shrewdly, and with extraordinary cunning". It was to his ears music of austerity, it should be added, but it was "music of impressive austerity, of true character; music bold in outline and of singular power".

But Mr. Gilman's voice was a fairly isolated one that day in the New York press. Mr. Henderson pursued his old line of attacking the Concerto's modernism. Samuel Chotzinoff of the World resented the trespass on Gershwin's domain, and Olin Downes of the New York Times criticized on formal grounds the abrupt, interrupting devices that were precisely contrived to evoke primitive "hot" jazz. "It progresses", Mr. Downes wrote, "by fits and starts, impressing the listener anew with the talent of the composer and confirming his suspicions that Mr. Copland needs a firmer hold of principles of musical structure than he has before he will do his own ideas justice. Here is a young man who can surely not remain content with the praise of partisans or knowledge of his own artistic shortcomings."

But a lonely voice in the powerful New York press, and especially the voice of a man so highly respected as Lawrence Gilman, was far better than none. And violent dissent among audiences was better than apathy. It indicated that Copland's music meant enough to a sufficiently large part of the public for them to get excited about it. And whatever the reaction of the press, and however strong the antagonism towards "hot" jazz among listeners at large, there were still enough people who reacted favorably to the vernacular elements of Copland's music to make it attractive, despite Mr. Downes's claim, to more than just "partisans".

With the *Ode,* however, things became somewhat different. Mr. Parker, who by that time could be regarded as a member of the innermost circle, remained faithful. But Mr. Gilman experienced a change of heart:

It was my pleasure and privilege to praise Mr. Copland's widely execrated Piano Concerto when it was played five years ago. But in comparison with that gusty and joyously challenging work, the new Ode is, for the most part, impotent and unrewarding . . . Hearing it, one visions Mr. Copland lost in agonizing lucubration, praying Heaven to make him Hard and Stripped and Sharp-Edged and Astringent and all the other things that a composer must learn to be in order to escape the sin of sensibility. [Mar. 4, 1932]

Austerity, the presence of which in the Concerto Gilman had admitted, was thoroughly tolerable to him so long as it operated upon demotic material (jazz) that was in itself not austere, that was, rather, wild and unleashed. In the *Ode,* jazz was still an inspiring agent. The work is, in fact, an expansion, by means of the variation form, of the blues motif of an earlier Nocturne for violin and piano. But jazz elements around this time in Copland's development start to become screened behind more general musical devices and they alternate with subject matter that has nothing to do with jazz. By the time of the Piano Variations, which followed the *Ode,* jazz in any strict sense is sifted out entirely, and what remains of it is idealized to a point where it is no longer recognizable.

If the *Ode* is a transitional work, in the Variations Copland's esoteric style—"esoteric", that is to say, in a relative sense or in the eyes of the broader musical public —emerges completely crystallized. Within modern-music circles this extraordinary piano work made a profound impression, and went a long way towards establishing him as a composer of great consequence. Outside of these circles, it was regarded as somewhat freakish and inaccessible, and hardly a reference to it was unaccompanied by the epithet, "austere". To this day it is considered forbidding and its appeal is confined to relatively few, though its importance in Copland's development and the development of music in general, as we shall later see, is very considerable indeed.

All is well with an esoteric style as long as you confine yourself to solo and chamber works, which are about as much as the modern-music societies, deprived of the monetary backing of the big combines, can afford. But if you have cultivated such a style, trouble starts when you write for symphony orchestra. Thus, Copland's first effort for large orchestra in his new style, the *Short Symphony* (1933), a work that must be included among his masterpieces, was scheduled for performance by more than one eminent conductor, but found too taxing for players and potential listeners as the performance dates drew near. The risk was too great when so much expense was involved. Extra rehearsals would be required, and even if the music were an artistic success, the box-office would suffer.

In the United States the work gathered dust on the shelf until 1944, when Stokowski and the National Broadcasting Company Symphony gave it its only performance in this country to date. It was, however, presented by Chávez, in 1934, and twice more since then, in Mexico—the country, as it happens, where Copland had gone to find the quiet and detachment necessary for absorbing himself in the working out of his new, tenuous idiom. *Statements* (1934), the next work in this idiom, though still fairly difficult for average listeners, was less difficult for the players, but even so, only two movements were played at its first performance, two years after its completion. The *Short Symphony* was rescored for sextet in 1937, and in this form it is occasionally heard.

## Appeal to a Wider Public

Experiences like the one with the *Short Symphony* understandably led Copland to a drastic revision of attitude in the middle 'thirties. Orchestral music for limited audiences was a contradiction in terms, as he began to realize, since orchestras are maintained by and for large groups. And so it was that he sought a new plan:

> During these years I began to feel an increasing dissatisfaction with the relations of the music-loving public and the living composer. The old "special" public of the modern music concerts had fallen away, and the conventional concert public continued apathetic or indifferent to anything but the

established classics. It seemed to me that we composers were in danger of working in a vacuum. Moreover, an entirely new public for music had grown up around the radio and phonograph. It made no sense to ignore them and to continue writing as if they did not exist. I felt that it was worth the effort to see if I couldn't say what I had to say in the simplest possible terms.

Conversations with his friend, Virgil Thomson, reinforced this point of view. Thomson, with his passion for Satie's music, insisted there was room for a more relaxed type of art in addition to that which strained for the maximum intricacy in every bar. Such music would not, moreover, merely by virtue of its simplicity, be obliged to relax standards of taste, value, and imagination. Thomson's opera, *Four Saints in Three Acts,* demonstrated, in 1934, how effectively it could appeal to a wider audience without letting down the cognoscenti.

The trend towards simplification was, to be sure, part of a much broader international movement. In Russia, Shostakovitch was criticized in the early 'thirties for his lack of simplicity. In Germany, the trend took the form of the powerful *Gebrauchsmusik* movement, with Paul Hindemith as its mentor. In 1937, this general trend, in its American manifestations, was reinforced by *The Cradle Will Rock*—a cross between opera and musical comedy by Marc Blitzstein, who is indebted to Copland for some of the earliest performances of his works at Yaddo and the League of Composers, at a time when he too, like Copland, had been writing austere and relatively esoteric music.

It was not only simplification that created a broader demand for Copland's music, but also the serviceability he now aimed for. The two were, of course, related, since simplification acted as a means of access to such practical spheres as radio (*Music for Radio*), schools (*Outdoor Overture* and *Second Hurricane*), movies (*Of Mice and Men, North Star,* etc.), and ballet (*Billy the Kid, Rodeo,* etc.).

Copland's previous work for the theater had been limited to incidental music for *Miracle at Verdun* in 1931. (*Grohg* can scarcely be counted, since it was not for an actual production, and *Music for the Theater* was a commentary on this genre rather than for specific use.) Thus, it was not until the middle 'thirties that Copland placed his music, to a substantial degree, at the service of any of the allied fields of art. But he was never a stranger to any of these allied fields. His wide intellectual and artistic interests go back to his youth and he had, moreover, always associated very closely with practitioners of the other arts. When he returned in 1924 from his first visit to Paris he had been accepted as one of the "season's favorite musical celebrities", to quote again from Clurman, who recalls, in this connection, being dragged along by his composer friend to a private party at which "people like" Albert Einstein, Mae West, Paul Robeson, Ferenc Molnar, Carl Van Vechten, and Albert Coates were gathered in one room.[1] In the early 'thirties, when Clurman founded the Group Theater, Copland had a still more rigorous means of keeping in touch with the aims and activities of those in other fields. The Group Theater was more than a play-giving unit. Connected with it were discussion meetings that acted as a sounding-board for ideologies of the time and that bore some distant relationship to the sort of thing Copland encouraged informally in the Young Composers Group about the same time. Representatives of various arts—all of these arts, of course, inevitably allied to the theater by nature—convened with playwrights like Clifford Odets. Such artists included Waldo Frank, novelist; Ralph Steiner, photographer; William Lescaze, architect, to mention but a small minority. Among them Copland figured as emissary from the musical domain.

It was from these associations that he received important impetus for his whole general musical tendency at this point of his career. It seems hardly accidental that his turn towards simplification and a broader audience should coincide with the later depression years, when artists and

---

1 Clurman, *op. cit.*, p. 14.

intellectuals who had formerly been escapist became aware of politics and economics. Liberalism as a means to social recovery became a central topic of discussion among intellectuals. It was important to come out of the shell, to think of the plight of the people, and this was one of the principles that guided the productions of the Group Theater. Such ideas achieved a still wider sphere of influence in the activities of the Works Progress Administration Theater, itself a product of the depression that had brought this mode of thinking in its wake. The people were not only to be the source of subject matter for works of art, but these works were to be simple enough in means, direct and immediate enough in appeal, for the common man to recognize in them himself and his problems.

Liberal thinking has often accompanied the humanism and the idealistic outlook of creative individuals, as we may observe without any difficulty if we look back upon the history of the masters in all artistic fields. The directions in which their aspirations turned did not always prove, in the end, to be conducive to the realization of these hopes—for example, Beethoven and his shattered expectations with regard to Napoleon. But an artist looks for something on which to fasten these aspirations, and for Copland's generation, in the 'thirties, the New Deal provided it.

The vein of optimism and patriotic sentiment, formerly confined to Rotarians and conservative artists, became *the thing* in the ranks of the *avant-garde,* and even composers who were unaware of the sociological origins fell in line, responding to what they thought was a purely creative trend. In their cries of "America I love you", beating their breasts, they sometimes outdid the Rotarians. Copland has never gone to this extreme, but came precariously close to it in *Lincoln Portrait.*

## The Years of Success

The new course adopted by Copland in the mid-'thirties has in it an element of reversion to an earlier stage of his evolution—for instance, in its incorporation of jazz elements again. But there is an important difference between his approach to these elements now and his approach a decade earlier: jazz now enters as merely a part, and a relatively small one, of broad American folk sources, which offered at once an extraordinarily plastic body of raw sonorous material for artistic treatment and a reliable means for engaging the interest of a wider audience.

Jazz elements in a cabaret scene for Ruth Page's ballet, *Hear Ye! Hear Ye!,* and the general theatrical serviceability of this work, mark the transition from the more abstract world. But this rapidly executed commission of 1934, pieced together in part from earlier material that had been in his sketchbook for years, disappeared from the repertory after its initial Chicago and New York performances. (A charming and piquant little blues from it was later published as the second of Copland's series of *Four Blues.*) It would thus seem, as a whole, to have no major significance in his output.

It was, rather, *El Salón México,* completed in 1934 (orchestrated in 1936), and *The Second Hurricane,* completed in 1937, that developed and heralded his new style. *The Second Hurricane,* described by its composer as a "play-opera for high school students", was perhaps the more crucial, since it was the one that thoroughly convinced him the new style was worth pursuing further. The concrete form of contact it provided for him with the non-professionals who performed it, and the aspect of youngsters having fun out of making music, gave him no end of delight. He knew beyond doubt that this simplification of means was eminently worth striving for.

*El Salón México,* however, did the important work of bringing the new style to the attention of a wide concert and radio public, of winning the popularity towards which this whole tendency aimed, and establishing Copland as a definitely "successful" composer. The reception of this work in London at a festival of the International Society for Contemporary Music was a particularly brilliant one, and was in some ways a turning-point for Copland. It was after this occasion that Boosey and Hawkes gave him a long-term contract, assuring the publication of each new work soon after its completion.

*El Salón México* does not belong to the category of works written expressly for theater, schools, or other function. But its aims were similar: to refer beyond the realm of absolute music and thus provide some bridge to the music itself for listeners with limited capacity for formal or technical perception. The gap between Copland's theater and concert works was more specifically bridged in 1942 by *Lincoln Portrait,* which brings a speaker into the concert hall to recite words of the great emancipator.

It is symptomatic that Copland should have been interested in writing his books, *What to Listen for in Music,* published in 1939, and *Our New Music,* published in 1941, during the early years of his appeal to a larger public. For both of these are addressed to laymen in an attempt to educate them musically, and thus helped consolidate his position with such listeners not only by enlarging the audience for music in general—and his music as a part of it—but also by bringing his name to the attention of a greater number of people. Both books have enjoyed a considerable success, and the second has been widely read in South America in a Spanish translation, and has had two different translations in German, one published in Vienna and one in Munich.

Copland's success with a more extensive public inevitably brought with it recognition from certain big-league, official quarters. Imposing benefits followed in rapid succession: a Columbia Broadcasting System commission (for *Music for Radio,* 1937), selection by the Music Educators National Conference of his *Outdoor Overture* for inclusion in the recommended list of contest repertory for school orchestras, election to the National Institute of Arts and Letters in 1942, the Pulitzer Prize in music in 1945 for *Appalachian Spring,* and awards from the New York Music Critics Circle, in 1945 for *Appalachian Spring* and in 1947 for the Third Symphony. He also received the Motion Picture Academy award in 1950, for his music for *The Heiress.* (This list of honors is by no means complete.) And he enjoyed an uncommon luxury for any serious American composer when *Lincoln Portrait* was issued on disks almost simultaneously by Victor and Columbia.

In the decade following 1935 Copland did not entirely give up writing abstract works even though his preoccupation was, as we have seen, with a medium associated with some functional or deliberately self-imposed external matter, without being programmatic in the 19th-century sense. As early as 1935, while he was teaching at Harvard and orchestrating *El Salón México,* he already had sketches for his Piano Sonata, which he resumed in 1939, completing it in Chile in 1941. In 1943, he completed his Sonata for Violin and Piano, stealing moments for its composition while working on a Hollywood lot for *North Star,* when his time was not required by the studio. Both sonatas loom high in his output. Rather than slighting them because they are not for large orchestra, as many composers today are likely to do, he took advantage of the fact that they would not be at the mercy of commercial forces of orchestras, radio, etc., and put some of his most earnest effort into them.

It was not, however, until his Third Symphony, commissioned by the Koussevitzky Foundation, that he returned to orchestral music without any extra-musical strings attached—if I may be allowed the pun. It was a grave and decisive point in his career, since he had directed his orchestral efforts towards other spheres for so long. When he had completed his semester at Harvard in June 1944, he drove to Mexico again, as if to find for his new symphony somewhat the same secluded atmosphere that had been favorable to his most ambitious earlier orchestral work in absolute form, the *Short Symphony.* Anxious once again to cut himself off from the practical world in which he had become so inextricably, though willingly, involved, he sought the seclusion of Tepotzlan, where no white man had lived since Robert Redfield wrote a book about it (after spending eight months there in the middle 'thirties) and where newspapers, radios, telephones, and telegrams are still the exception. There he remained through October. The following March he retreated again, this time no farther than Bernardsville, N. J., and stayed there until October, finishing the first two movements of the symphony. While working there on his symphony he found time to relax from the strain by tossing off a score for an Office of War Information documentary film, *The Cummington Story*. In a converted barn in Richmond, Mass., near Tanglewood, the symphony was completed on September 29, 1946.

A commission from the Elizabeth Sprague Coolidge Foundation for a work to be performed in 1950 at the Foundation's twenty-fifth anniversary festival gave Copland further opportunity to turn his efforts, in a quartet for piano and strings, in the direction of a more abstract form of music. As to the two-movement clarinet concerto for Benny Goodman, begun in Rio de Janeiro in 1947 and completed in the United States October 1948, it too is abstract in a way, though there may be some who will question this characterization, since the piece evokes at times Goodman's own style of sophisticated jazz.

Settings of twelve poems of Emily Dickinson occupied Copland from March, 1949, to March, 1950. Following them his attention was deflected from composition for a while by his preparations for the Norton lectures at Harvard University, which comprise his book, *Music and Imagination*. In 1952 Copland's friends became aware that he had some works in progress (among them, an opera and a fantasy for piano), but in his characteristic fashion he has remained non-committal about these incomplete projects.

*Part Two*

# THE MUSIC

# II

## The Stages of Copland's Development

Aaron Copland's style, in the course of thirty years, has undergone a series of striking transformations, determined partly by a rare critical faculty and partly by an unusual sense of responsibility to musical audiences. He is not of the line of artists who, after following a dubious creative urge, justify their course by saying merely that they "felt that way". Quite the contrary, he is capable of examining what he has accomplished as if from outside. And he has not hesitated to say, at certain turning-points of his career, that this or that tendency has been exploited by him for all it is worth, and that some new tactic is called for.

The phases of his evolution and the motivation for them have been indicated in Part One against the background of a professional career of wide scope. It would be logical for us now simply to retrace the same ground and analyze the stylistic traits of each period. But though the lines of demarcation between phases are in one sense distinguishable —and, indeed, obvious enough to anyone who has followed his progress—the works themselves resist rigorous separation into cubby-holes, because they are all distinguished by a pervasive and unmistakable individuality. There is more difference between his total output and the rest of the accumulated literature of music than there is between one chronological segment of his works and another. Even the workmanship and depth of substance of what is far too glibly segregated as his "workaday" music do not fall appreciably below the level he maintains in his more "serious" or more "abstract" works, and in several cases they are equal.

Also, Copland is of the school of slow, careful workers peculiar to our century, and a work that emerges at one point of his career is not unlikely to have had its inception several years earlier—as an example, the sketches in 1935 for the Piano Sonata he worked on from 1939 to 1941. Further overlapping results from the fact that each period, instead of being a brusque turnabout, involves often an increased interest in some aspect of his creative activity that had been present before.

It would seem, then, more strategic to deal with Copland's music without recourse to chronology. At the same time, it is convenient for the reader to keep the stages in mind, not because any given work will sound better with this knowledge, but in order that he may not interpret observations applicable to one period as applicable in the same degree to another. Let us review them briefly before proceeding.

To begin with, there was the formative stage every creative artist goes through, and this will be dismissed simply with the list of juvenilia in the appendix. What is more properly his "first style" gradually developed from 1920 to 1925. *The Cat and the Mouse* and the small works following mark both the end of his student period and the beginning of his professional career. *Grohg, As it fell upon a day,* and the Symphony for Organ and Orchestra are the chief works of this professional beginning. The emotional poles of his musical language are already established—a personal nostalgia and wiriness, with a liberal use of dissonance idiomatic of the 'twenties. European influences are present, but there is strong American flavor—not enough, however, to satisfy Copland in his subsequent phases.

Copland's second style came to the public's attention with *Music for the Theater* (1925). It is marked by a trend towards an indigenous idiom through incorporation of jazz. The Trio (1929) is a transition towards the increased leanness of texture and the intricate and abstract patterns distinguishing the works from the Piano Variations (1930) through *Statements* (1934).

The commission for the ballet, *Hear Ye! Hear Ye!*, turned Copland's attention in 1934 towards the theater and music for use. This period, characterized by an intense interest in folksong, seems to have endured the longest for Copland and to have provided an important solution for his creative aims. Paralleling his "workaday" music since that time, there has been a series of works in abstract form, ranging from the Piano Sonata (1941), commissioned by Clifford Odets, to the Piano Quartet (1950). With the Third Symphony (1946) the balance seems to have shifted in the direction of the more abstract works in which the gains from his contact with folk music are consolidated in new and larger forms. But it is too soon to say whether this is a new phase, reversion to an earlier phase, or, what is most likely, the arrival at an equilibrium that enables him to move easily from one genre to another.

## Copland's Economy of Means

With this blueprint of Copland's evolution in mind we may turn to more specific consideration of his music. What strikes analytical attention before almost anything else is his economy of means, the transparency of his textures, the preciseness of his tonal vocabulary—all of them rare accomplishments at a time when approximate effects are often considered sufficient because they seem to serve a composer's immediate ends in works heard from a distance in large concert halls. These qualities of workmanship are commonly thought to be virtues of the mind, which are anathema to contemporary critics, who assume that feeling is thus excluded. But Copland's economy is determined as much by an almost Romantic concern with expression as by the disciplined mentality of a sober artisan.

If this is not always apparent, it is because many people

still think of emotion in its 19th-century manifestation, which was pervasive, expansive, and mystically concerned with the nexus of things. Love, religion, infinity, destiny, the ocean, the aeolian harp, referred to vaguely and reverently with capital letters, were inevitably equated, and composers were carried along in a flood of mingled sensations. In Copland, on the other hand, one is immediately aware of control, through which he aims at a mood's essence, after paring away ramifications and the accidental. In his rarefied efforts of the early 'thirties, what often came forward, contradictory as it may seem, resembled the skeleton of feeling more than feeling itself. Romantic attitudes appeared in a strange new light. As early as 1929, Paul Rosenfeld keenly observed:

> The earmark of Copland's music is leanness, slenderness of sound, sharpened by the fact that it is found in connection with a strain of grandiosity. For we associate grandiosity with a Wagnerian fatness, thickness, and heaviness; and Copland's [piano] concerto, and the finale of his [first] symphony . . . give us the pleasant shock of finding it both lithe and imponderous.[1]

Though Copland's style has undergone many changes since this statement was made, the combination of leanness and a certain grandiosity is still one of the things that invest his music with a quite special and intriguing quality. In the case of his massive Third Symphony, this Romantic element seems to stem from Mahler rather than Wagner. Mahler, in fact, has always been one of Copland's favorite composers, which would seem odd for anyone so thoroughly oriented towards the incisive, economical, and athletic idioms of our time. At one point in his career, he went so far as to write an indignant letter to the New York Times (April 2, 1925) deploring the apathy of critics and conductors towards this Austrian symphonist. "That Mahler has on occasion been grandiloquent is undeniable", he admitted, and further, "Mahler has possibly never written a perfect masterpiece." But, he concludes, "In my opinion,

---

[1] *An Hour with American Music,* Philadelphia, 1929, p. 128.

such things as the first movement of the Seventh Symphony, the scherzo of the Ninth, the last movement of the Fourth, and the entire *Das Lied von der Erde* have in them the stuff of living music."

Copland seems concerned with personalizing whatever he manipulates. Everything is excluded that does not directly conform with sentiments he himself has experienced. The universal stock-in-trade (scales, arpeggios, sonorities that merely fill in) he usually avoids, though less so nowadays. From 1925 to 1934 he was, as a matter of fact, largely occupied with weeding out just such paraphernalia. Something like arpeggios exists in the Piano Concerto. *Vitebsk,* his trio, in which his more recent gaunt, exposed dissonances make one of their earliest appearances, contains scalewise passages. But personal ingredients were strong—were, indeed, astonishingly present almost from the start—as, for example, in the agreeable setting of *As it fell upon a day* of 1923:

This concern over using only his own material (though not in the narrow sense of the futurists who create an incommunicable world) and only the notes relevant to a given feeling context, is a part of what makes him the slow, careful worker I have already described him to be. He lives with any composing project until he is sure the result is, or has become through re-molding, entirely his own.

Living with a work himself, especially where larger forms are concerned, he can be sure, moreover, that other people may live with it and derive increased enjoyment. Like Stravinsky (though both toss off little works by the wayside), he is essentially a one-work-a-year composer, if the bigger efforts and the dates of completion are taken into account. At a recent meeting between these two composers, they casually compared notes. Both of them had every reason to feel confident of their ability to write rapidly if they so desired. Copland has proved how well he can do so in many commissions rapidly executed for specific occasions since 1934. But with a more serious work, they agreed, it is better to see for themselves how well it wears, rather than shift this burden to the public. "I like to feel comfortable with it", said Stravinsky, adjusting his jacket over his shoulders as one might do with a garment still too new to have assumed the body's shape and a familiar, supple feel. To this Copland fervently nodded his assent.

Economy of means went very well with a leaning towards French style that characterized such early Copland products as *The Cat and the Mouse* and the Passacaglia. It is interesting in this regard to note that the leaning was strongly present before he went abroad, while he was under the tutelage of a musician so inclined towards mid-European sources as Rubin Goldmark. In Paris, as we have seen above, Copland was exposed to many influences besides the French and his style modified itself accordingly. But all in all it may be safely said that the European roots cultivated in Copland's music during the 'twenties were predominantly Parisian.

One sometimes spoke in those days of a "Brooklyn Stravinsky". Today this seems curious, with both composers better known. Did one mean Stravinsky was a springboard for the younger man's autonomous development? If so, who could serve this function better for someone of Copland's lucidity? True, the future of the primitivist idiom of *Le Sacre* and *Les Noces* was limited. But the principles enunciated in the *Octuor* (1923) of the Russian master were enormously plastic. One may marvel at the power of the originator to suggest to Copland a point of departure from which to proceed, in a very short time, to the remarkable individuality of the Piano Variations of 1930.

## The Variations as Focal Point

The Variations occupy a crucial position in Copland's evolution. If I dwell on them at this juncture, it is because they are a vantage point from which to look in both directions. The lonely meditative strain harks back to the nostalgic "blues" of his earlier music. The peremptory tone, the rhetoric, look forward to the Piano Sonata, and to the imperious introduction of *Billy the Kid* preparing us for the epic tale of a well-meaning desperado. As an example of Copland's conciseness we could scarcely find anything better than the Variations, and the degree of this conciseness in itself affords us the means of observing his musical devices in their most pristine state.

The impression these Variations made in the early 'thirties was profound and exciting. This was one of those instances when what Jacques Maritain calls a "new type-analogy of the beautiful" seemed to have been revealed to us—namely, a new way of re-arranging existing musical materials to make "the brilliance of form. . . shine upon matter", "a new adaptation of the first and eternal rules, and even the use of *viae certae et determinatae* not hitherto employed, which are at first disconcerting".[1] There were outer similarities to the variations of Stravinsky's *Octuor* (compare the thematic fragments of Exx. 2A and 2C, and of 2B with 2D), and there were affinities to the piano style of Bartók (notably of his Piano Sonata), to whom Copland showed himself devoted in some lectures given at the New School for Social Research, during the period when the Variations were written. And there were also methods of thematic treatment in which Copland must have received impetus from Schoenberg's contribution to our century. But essentially the work was like nothing ever conceived before.

---

[1] *Art and Scholasticism*, London, 1934, p. 46 (translation of *Art et Scolastique*, 1927).

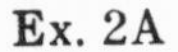

Ex. 2A

Copland, Piano Variations: Theme

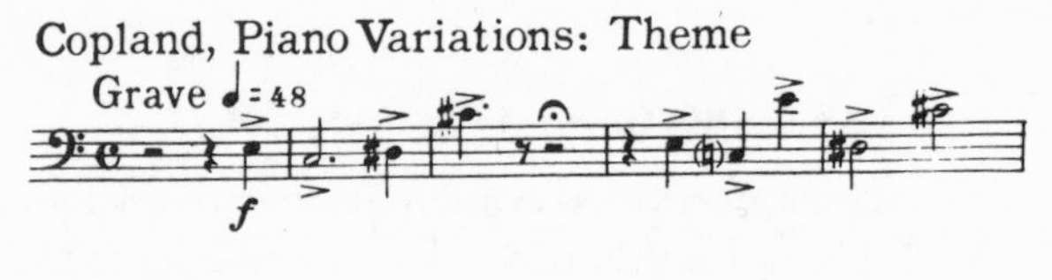


B

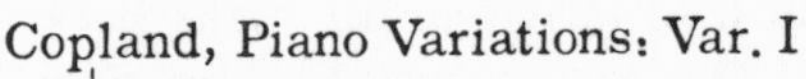

Copland, Piano Variations: Var. I

C

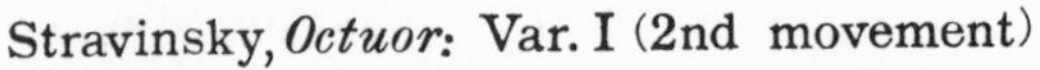

Stravinsky, *Octuor:* Var. I (2nd movement)

D

Stravinsky, *Octuor:* Theme
(2nd movement)

It was in its second performance, at a Yaddo festival, where I first heard it, that it really took fire, partly, no doubt, because this was a gathering of the élite of America's modern-music circles. Rosenfeld's account of the provocative event keeps it vividly present.[1]

The stony eloquence of American urbanism seemed to me very odd indeed against the background of Yaddo's Gothic hall and the Saratoga landscape outside. The concentration of the music and of Copland's performance was compelling. He dwelt on every tone, as if to distil the last

[1] *Discoveries of a Music Critic,* New York, 1936, pp. 357-59.

ounce of sonority out of it—which was as it should be, since there were so few tones. (This style sets the pattern for the performance of all his piano works, which seem to depend somehow on the resonance lingering between the striking of one key and the next.) The structure was an achievement—variations without the episodic character that limits even some works of the old masters in this form. The theme (given in its entirety in Ex. 3) contained tones that were used for all they were worth by the time the work was over. Each chord or figure may be traced directly back to it.

Ex. 3

If only for this aspect, the work is a masterpiece of construction. But more remarkable is the exciting character of the transmutations when heard. Devices erudite as these on paper do not always translate themselves so effectively into sound. The methods of motif transformation in particular, which Copland shares with Schoenberg, are not, when Copland applies them, the intellectual exercises they may be in works of some of the rigorous followers of the Viennese master. Chief among these methods is the variation of a fixed set of notes by transposing one or more of them an octave (sometimes even two or more octaves) above or below. The procedure is not original with Schoenberg, as we may gather from Beethoven's treatment of the words *"Seid umschlungen, Millionen!"* in the Ninth Symphony first in spread form, then in simplified contraction:

By this method, for example, the series of notes in the opening motif of Schoenberg's Suite, Op. 25 (Ex. 5A), is transformed to take the shape, at the opening of the second movement, of the phrase in Ex. 5B:

Copland's application of this device is illustrated by the metamorphosis the tones of Ex. 2A go through when they recur in Ex. 2B, and the changes are continually rung on this process with inexhaustible imagination as the work continues. The theme itself is constructed by repetition of the original tones with interpolations—for example, the E at the end of the fourth measure, and much more elaborate insertions in the latter half of the theme. Such devices, of course, place Copland's procedure outside the realm of twelve-tone music. But the way in which he stays close to his original "tone-row", if we may borrow the expression, is evocative of that music.

The method of constructing longer melodic lines out of short, nuclear elements by interpolation or extension has remained Copland's characteristic way. Observe, for example, the opening of the Violin Sonata (1943):

Ex. 6

The direct relating of almost every note back to the theme of the Variations, and thus ultimately to the first four notes, is illustrated by Variation II (Ex. 7A), where the notes not only provide, re-arranged, a counterpoint or harmony in the lowest voice, but (in the treble) an accompanying figure as well. Where the notes do not relate back directly, they are clearly interpolated into the original phrase according to the method we have already observed in the construction of the theme. Thus, in Variation XV the theme in quarter notes is accompanied by a version of itself in eighth notes which is derived through interpolations and redisposition (Ex. 7B).

One thing must be emphasized before leaving the discussion of this work. Those elements that hark back to Schoenberg, Stravinsky, or Bartók in no sense render it eclectic, but, on the contrary, enrich it since they are all part of a normal evolution, and are thoroughly absorbed in an eminently personal idiom. There are also origins in jazz which, though entirely American in their manifestations, go back, perhaps, more to Milhaud than, as is sometimes suggested, to Gershwin. It is more likely that Gershwin's motivations arose out of the same source as Copland's (namely, out of Milhaud) than that Gershwin influenced Copland. Jazz was in the atmosphere to which both were exposed, and its embodiment in serious music had already been strikingly achieved by composers in France.

## Jazz Influences

The Variations present in crystallized form an idiom that had made itself fairly well felt in the *Symphonic Ode,* where Copland had begun to reject the more literal references to jazz while preserving some of its more vital features. In his autobiographical sketch, Copland has observed:

> With the Concerto I felt I had done all I could with the idiom, considering its limited scope. True, it was an easy way to be American in musical terms, but all American music could not possibly be confined to two dominant moods: the "blues" and the snappy number. The characteristic rhythmic element of jazz . . . being independent of mood, yet purely indigenous, will undoubtedly continue to be used in serious native music.

Writing about jazz at an earlier date,[1] he had reduced this element to a division of eighth notes of a 4/4 measure into groups of three and five. His use of this device in serious music is clearly exemplified as early as 1923 in the Rondino of the Two Pieces for String Quartet:

Ex. 8

which serves to remind us that his later jazz period was not the result of an arbitrary decision. There were obvious predispositions towards it almost from the beginning.

In the *Symphonic Ode,* this rhythmic pattern still makes its appearance in fairly literal form (Ex. 9A). But by the time of the Variations, the 5/8, by extension of the principle, is abstracted from duple or fox-trot meter while preserving some of the aura of jazz syncopation (Ex. 9B).

Ex. 9 A

[1] *Jazz Structure and Influence,* in *Modern Music,* Jan. 1927, and in *Our New Music,* p. 89 ff.

Ex. 9 B

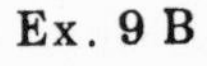

More general types of syncopation, equally suggestive of jazz, are still to be found today in Copland's music, but the developments to which they are subjected often remove them very far indeed from the character of their source.

Also available to the serious artist is the alternating major and minor third of "blues" quoted literally in *Music for the Theater,* a work that deliberately takes the clichés of the 'twenties and heightens them in a way that makes them still arresting (Ex. 10A). In the passage from the Prelude of the First Symphony (Ex. 10B), an earlier work, the F (indicated by *x*) gave some of the same suggestion of an alternate major third in relation to the C-sharp.

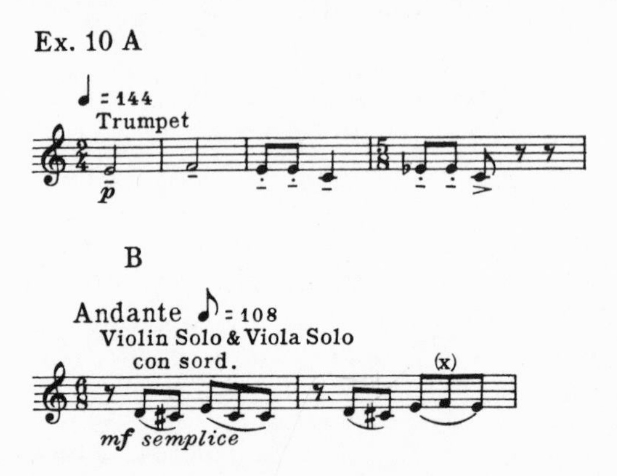


What had happened in the years of *Music for the Theater* and the Piano Concerto was merely that these and other jazz suggestions became more frequent and overt. With the Variations such devices become very complex, much idealized, and almost unrecognizable. Thus in the opening section, although I do not think Copland consciously planned it, there is an intricate dovetailing of this major-minor suggestion on three different chords without being polytonal. The first three notes (Ex. 3), if D-sharp is heard as E-flat, parenthetically suggest the blues-figure in C—an ambiguity that is reinforced in the tenth measure by the C major-minor chord. But the theme is in C-sharp minor. B-sharp, notated in the second measure as C to allow for this ambiguity, also (as C) serves as the alternate minor third of the A-major chord in the third measure.

Used melodically, thirds often point to jazz origin in Copland even without the modal duplicity. The interval is, in fact, his trademark—notably in its descending form, in which the blues element is stressed. An amazing number of movements start with it, and it is often set in relief by the pause on the lower note, as in the Variations. It characteristically serves as a nucleus upon which melodic elements build by accretion. It may, in its first appearance, be adorned by neighbor notes, but its span is somehow outlined from the very start. By the method of octave-transposition of single notes I have described above, thirds often become tenths either through variation of a given theme or in their original presentation. With reference to Copland's use of the tenth, Theodore Chanler, after many compliments for the *Symphonic Ode,* observed:

> It cannot be denied that certain uses he puts it to make one see something in this interval, in its color, that one never saw before. But at other times there seems to be no . . . reason at all for using it, except to be consistent.[1]

Since the early 'thirties, Copland has broadened the sphere of his melodic sources (notably by recourse to regional folk music) so that by now his music embraces many intervallic contours besides the third and tenth. But these intervals have remained prominent nonetheless.

---

[1] Henry Cowell, ed., *American Composers on American Music,* Stanford University, Calif., 1933, p. 52.

## Declamatory Style

It is not at all implausible that the "blues", besides affecting the intervallic shape of Copland's melody, has also had something to do with the declamatory style so characteristic of his writing. A brooding quality in "blues" arises not only out of the minor mode and its emphasis by contrast of occasional major thirds, but also out of the return at each phrase-end to an often prolonged home-tone, which points up the feeling of resignation. In place of the arch of traditional melody that starts at one point and progresses to another, or returns after excursion, it is more usual to find in Copland's music a kind of impassioned speech in tones, a broad recitative revolving about a fixed point—a recitative in which the "blues" has become so transformed that we would not, perhaps, recognize it as a possible source were it not for the clue provided by the major-minor thirds.

Other sources, equally elusive, have no doubt also entered into the formation of Copland's special type of declamation, among them the psalmodic chants of the synagogue with their biblical air of prophecy and gloom. Copland's Trio, *Vitebsk,* subtitled "Study on a Jewish Theme", is his only work deliberately embodying Jewish material. (Quarter-tones, suggesting somewhat the portamento of oriental vocal style, have an incidental role in this work, but never recur in his music.) But from time to time, and often where we least expect it, a Hebraic suggestion is not unlikely to enter. A case in point is the repeated-note phrase that occurs quite in passing in the Lento of the *Short Symphony* (Ex. 11A), suggesting a cantor's lament. Later, in *Quiet City,* the phrase is much more prominent and evocative (Ex. 11B), and specifically motivated here by a Jewish element that enters into the play for which this score was written.

Ex. 11 A

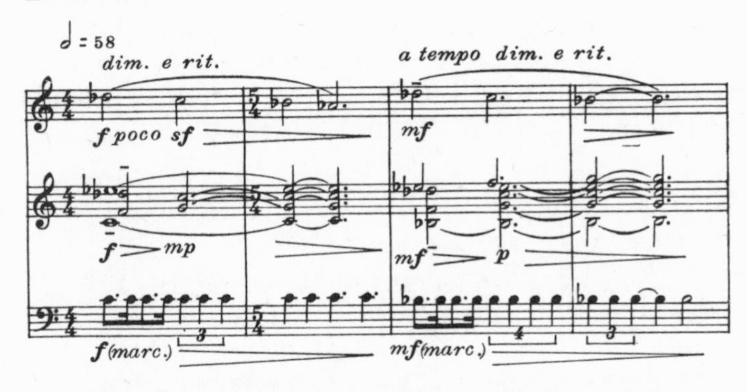


B

The declamatory style is but an elaboration of this chant-like dwelling on a single note. The note-repetitions are modified by little deviations from the horizontal plane. Short groups of notes of moderate duration (often approximately two note-lengths, shorts and longs—for example, quarters and halves in Ex. 3) are separated by a recurrent element of longer duration. The recurrent element may be either a single note—an integral part of the melody—or a punctuating, accompanying chord between the phrases. In Ex. 3 the recurring C-sharps are part of the melody, but the percussive chords in measures 3 and 10 have two notes in common that also convey something of a recurrent punctuation, so that both versions of the device are exemplified. The differences between the two chords reflect the artist embroidering on the given pattern. We may observe the device further, and the methods of embroidering upon it, in the fourth movement, *Subjective,* of *Statements* (Ex. 12), where E recurs sometimes as part of a punctuating chord (*x*), sometimes in a chord beginning a new phrase (*y*), sometimes alone (*z*). If one follows this movement through, the many deviations Copland ingeniously imposes on the basic plan may be very well estimated. (See also the D's in Ex. 6 as an instance of a similar recurrence.)

Ex. 12

In more recent years, since Copland has had recourse to folk music, declamatory style often gives way to what we more familiarly know as melody. But a new type of declamation also has entered, deriving from the various forms of American hymnody that he has added to his musical vocabulary. It is for the musicologists to determine precisely where each colloquial or religious source is suggested in Copland's output. For us here it is enough to recognize that a composer who is predisposed to declamatory style, whether of the synagogue or jazz, may quite understandably be drawn to it when it reveals itself in a New England hymn. And let us not forget that New England and Hebrew psalmody have this in common: both are sacred forms.

When the type of melodic construction characteristic of declamatory style is employed in rapid music, the result is something quite different—toccata rather than declamation. The Allegro portion of the first movement of the Piano Sonata, with its recurring octaves on A, is a case in point (Ex. 13A), and this toccata style may also be observed at the opening of the Vivace of the same work (Ex. 13B), where two sixths instead of one note or chord serve as punctuation. Its most remarkable manifestation is at the opening of the *Short Symphony,* a provocative passage at

once playful and frantic, verging on the neurotic (Ex. 13C). The punctuating element is a kind of broken-chord figure (measures 2, 5, 7, and 13) in which the sixth, F-sharp to D, is prominent.[1]

[1] The Sextet arrangement of this symphony seemed for a while virtually to have supplanted the original orchestral version.

## Copland's Use of Folk Music

Copland's declamatory style, with its periodic return to a more or less fixed element, makes for a certain level character and, in slow movements especially, quite personal immobility. The more fluid melody that resulted when Copland turned to folk music was thus a welcome thing, for, however individual and striking this immobility may have been, it was not anything that could be fruitfully developed to the exclusion of other types of phrase-structure.

The evolution of a more fluid melody was not, however, Copland's motive for turning to folk music. It was, rather, as we saw in Part One, an aspect of his campaign to achieve a simple style and a content that would engage the interest of a wider audience. The Copland who could go to extremes of austerity, taxing at times even to some *avant-garde* listeners, now showed that he could also resort to disarming extremes of simplicity. The *Hoe-Down* from *Rodeo* and the slow section from *El Salón México* are virtually photographic, and seem to be more significant as records of certain contemporary popular genres than episodes to engage the intellectual fancy. But then to our astonishment we find in the same music such intricate developments as in *Buckaroo Holiday* in the first of these works, and, in the second, the fast closing-section that recalls the complex finale of the *Short Symphony*. And these are only two of many instances in which the music of this period pointed back to an earlier period in his evolution.

In his treatment of folk music Copland has grasped with extraordinary success its precise and essential curve, both where he quotes directly and where he creates original tunes along traditional lines of folksong. But it would be a gross simplification to say that he is no more than a skilled folklorist, a compiler of Baedekers for his continent, just as in the 'twenties it would have been unjust to cite him as merely a high-class representative of Tin Pan Alley. For, in the handling of folk patterns, Copland is capable of an exceptional degree of selectivity, transformation, and abstraction through which the essence of the material as well as a specific attitude, heightened emotion, ingenuity, and personality are conveyed. And it is precisely the skill he had acquired in dealing with abstract materials around 1930 that made it possible for him to achieve these qualities with folk music.

While his music of the 'forties profits from the many survivals of the sensitivity and expertness of an earlier period, there are, reciprocally, a fruitful new lyricism to condition the earlier contrived melodic fragments, and a new warmth to offset, as an additional element, the starkness and wiry athleticism. More human attitudes now animate the "tonal edifices" Paul Rosenfeld once found to "resemble nothing so much as steel cranes, bridges and the frames of skyscrapers".

In the early 'thirties it was rare for Copland to write anything that could be called a tune in the ordinary sense—something without the jagged large skips, something you could walk out of the hall whistling. I remember his childlike pleasure in such "finds" even as late as 1939, for example, the "Sunday Traffic Music" for *The City,* preserved in the suite, *Music for Movies:*

Ex. 14

It was all so new and fresh to him after his esoteric practices. Though no one, not even the composer himself, may take some of these ditties too seriously, they were part of a campaign to develop greater melodic skill.

In a sense, Copland's conversion of the middle 'thirties is not, as I have said, an altogether new one, for folk music now merely plays the role in his music that jazz (strictly speaking, also a form of folk music) had played in the 'twenties, and I have already indicated how jazz was later absorbed into a more serious style in the early 'thirties. The various types of folk music that have attracted Copland in more recent years have undergone an analogous evolution in his serious music. His *Danzón Cubano,* for example, stays quite close to the traditional Cuban pattern of the same name, but if we compare its main musical idea (Ex. 15A) with a passage in the Violin Sonata (Ex. 15B), we find a certain reflection, though the traditional Cuban pattern has become thoroughly idealized, and the relationship of the Violin Sonata to any popular form is very remote indeed.

Ex. 15 A

It is in the slow music in particular that the effect of folk music on Copland's more abstract works is revealed as a salutary one. Like many of his contemporaries Copland had relied upon rhythmic excitement for some of his effect. But this is obviously available mainly in rapid music. Thus, sustained movements tended towards a certain immobility of mood-painting, which could however rise to extraordinary beauty, as in the Lento of the *Short Symphony*. More recently, slow passages have been assuming a sharper profile, the profile often of melody derived from folk sources—the hymn in particular.

Having acquired this new ease in sustained, peaceful moods, Copland abuses it at times, as in the outer movements of the Piano Sonata, in which there is too much slow or moderately paced music. But one cannot deny the memorable inspirations like the elegiac close of that work, and it is indeed the restrained, beatific New England sorrow of the *Our Town* score that seems to be the chief source of this elegiac mood.

There are many such instances of folk influences on Copland's abstract works of recent years, but our aim now is to observe his procedures with folk music in works consciously devoted to such material. Copland contrives not only to invest the material with his own personality, but at the same time to place in relief the intrinsic properties that are, on the one hand, most striking in a purely musical way, and, on the other, most typical of the large genre of folk music of which the tune in question is a part.

One of his special devices in transforming a folksong is to make it broad or tender when it has been slight or frivolous originally, and in this way he brings out essences of which we were previously unaware. For example, in *Lincoln Portrait,* the comic song, *Springfield Mountain* (Ex.

Ex. 16 A

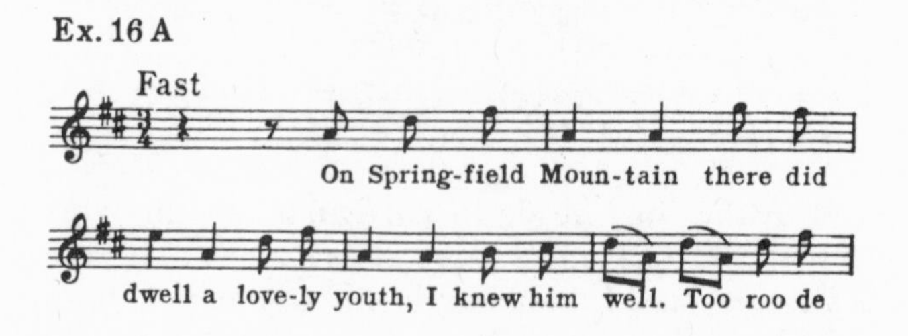

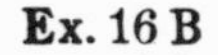

16A), is stretched out so that each one of its first few notes (Ex. 16B) occupies about the time of a whole measure of the original. Thus, a saucy ditty now expresses majesty. Further breadth is added by the time-spacing that results from lengthening the note at the end of each four-note group (at *x* in Ex. 16B). A final touch is the substitution (at *y* in Ex. 16B) of D for the more trite, scale-wise F-sharp.

In the ballet, *Billy the Kid,* the *pas de deux* of Billy and his sweetheart is based on another saucy air (Ex. 17A) which is similarly stretched out (Ex. 17B) to give it a tender quality:[1]

Ex. 17 A

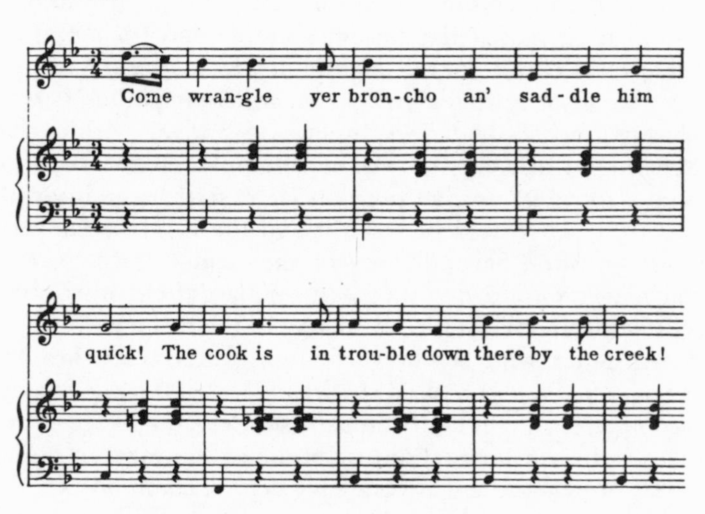


[1] This movement is included in the selections arranged for piano, but not in the orchestral suite.

Ex. 17 B

Note how skilfully the phrase is clipped at beginning and end. Note also how closely Copland, in the first six measures, adheres to the conventional accompaniment of the most common song collection. As we proceed, however, we observe the process of transformation at work. The accompaniment in particular becomes more venturesome. The supertonic chord in the eighth measure appears earlier than we had expected it, and its inherent pathos is emphasized not only by its premature arrival within the phrase, but also by the placing of the C in the bass an octave above its normal position (at *x*) so that the interval of a ninth is created between it and the B-flat of the previous measure. Several more of such contrivances in the course of the following six measures place these in striking relief against the simple orthodoxy of the first six.

A listener who is not very attentive, who catches an opening mood and basks drowsily in it until the movement is completed, might easily miss the subtlety, might see nothing but the sentimental setting of the earlier measures. Actually, however, these are but a segment of common experience that Copland has evoked merely to build upon subsequently—to introduce fruitful distortions bringing out the quality of the segment and giving it the special emphasis placed on part of the body in an inspired portrait where attention is thus focused on an essential property of the sitter, or a property that strikes the painter as significant. The ordinary observer, interested merely in a likeness, may either miss the emphasis or be disturbed by the fact that a limb is out of its normal position.

Displacement, as in Picasso's painting of the *Femme au bonnet rouge,* is, of course, only one of several contrivances a painter has at his disposal. Another familiar device, also disturbing to the layman, is disproportionate enlargement of a part of the body, as in Picasso's groups of nude women, painted in the early 'twenties. We have an exact correlative of this in Copland's use of the Mexican tune, *El Mosca,* in *El Salón México.* The tune is quite complex to start with (Ex. 18A) and the composer gets directly at the essence of its rhythmic complexity by drawing out still more the deviations from 6/8 time in the unconventionally long, syncopated notes in the second half of each measure (Ex. 18B). This is done by keeping the first three eighth notes intact (though the actual pitches are changed in terms of another Mexican theme), while further delaying the delayed notes of the second part of the measure. The result is a measure of 4/4.

Ex. 18 A

The ballet, *Rodeo,* also provides some fine instances of the emphasis of significant details. About half way through the first movement (*Buckaroo Holiday*), the trombone introduces *If he'd be a Buckaroo,* quoting the melody quite literally except for the spacing between the couplets:

Ex. 19

The original proceeds in regular quarters and eighths, but one extra half note at the close of the first couplet places the symmetry out of joint. Motivated by this deviation, Copland inserts still more protracted spacing between sections of the melody, in the form of several long grand-pauses of the full orchestra, each of them as many as two or more common-time measures in duration. The shock element of these protracted rests adds to the saucy character of the melody; and another element along similar lines is the lingering on two of the up-beats, in imitation of a common licence which ballad singers delight in taking. Earlier in the movement, there is ingenious play upon the short, clipped phrases of the second part of a tune called *Sis Joe.* Copland emphasizes the clipped quality by punctuating the phrases with loud drumbeats, and these beats give the impression of accents in a series of unequal measures, underlining the inherent inequality of the lengths of the short phrases which, in the original, had been given a certain symmetry through the metrical scheme.

It is easy to multiply examples of Copland's fertile manipulation of compiled source material, but the few given above may suffice to show why so much is to be gained from an intimacy with his music. From the relatively simple levels treated here it is possible to follow up the use of folk music through the instances of triple canons and contrapuntal combinations of two themes or of a theme with a part of itself as an accompaniment figure until we finally arrive at the exciting developments, such as the one at the end of *El Salón México,* where a motif compounded of fragments of two Mexican tunes is carried up in sequence to the giddy heights upon which the work comes to its brilliant conclusion.[1]

## The Rehabilitation of the Triad and Copland's Method of Chord-Building

One of the results of Copland's trend towards a simpler style has been the rehabilitation of the triad, the discovery of new harmonic possibilities afforded by its franker use. It is difficult to say whether this was a consequence of the folk music incorporated into his more recent works or whether the attractions the triad had for him determined to some extent his choice when he turned to folk music. Exploring Mexican music for *El Salón México,* for example, he found his attention arrested precisely by a chordal figure (Ex. 20A) occurring somewhere in the course of the tune, *El Palo Verde.* It is this figure, abstracted from its context, that we hear at the opening. Later the tune is heard in its complete form (Ex. 20B) and we become aware of how inspirational a touch the abstraction of this chordal figure has been—which is not to deny that

[1] See *Billy the Kid,* at No. 25a in the orchestral score, where the final motif of *Goodbye, Old Paint* becomes an *ostinato* in the woodwinds to accompany the repetition of the tune. See also the variations on *The Gift to be Simple* in *Appalachian Spring* (No. 55).

it is also arresting, in its striking orchestral dress, when first heard.

At another time, contemplating New England hymnody for the *Our Town* music, he was profoundly fascinated by the triadic contours that characterize this traditional source as a whole. There is only one instance in the film of literal quotation—a bit of Hollywood realism quite distinct from his contribution as score-writer, namely, the tune sung by the congregation in the sequence of the intoxicated church-organist. What Copland did for the most part was to extract from the raw material its idiomatic elements. These became so much a part of his own style that they soon were reflected in his abstract works, as I have already indicated with regard to the last movement of the Piano Sonata, in its evocation of the mood of the *Our Town* music. In the Violin Sonata the relationship is even more specific, as we may observe by comparing the following fragments:

This use of parallel triads a whole step apart has become quite a characteristic device with Copland, and it is one of the marks by which we may identify his influence in the music of several of our younger composers.

Reinforced by its contact with New England hymnody, the triad now runs a close second to the figure of the descending third, often being dwelt upon in the same formularized way. And this use of the triad melodically is only a by-product of its increased use in vertical harmony. Copland, I hasten to add, had never been one of those composers who abandoned the traditional formula altogether. The opening of the Lento from the Two Pieces for Strings is harmonized with simple parallel triads:

Ex. 22

But more usually, in the 'twenties and early 'thirties, interpolated tones, chromatic or otherwise, gave triadic harmonies complexity and dissonance. In the earlier years of the decade extending from 1925, his interpolations were likely to be frankly polytonal, as in such a strident passage as this:

Ex. 23

Piano Concerto

By the time of the *Ode,* a highly individual consistency of texture starts to emerge out of an integration of these accretions. That is to say, the notes that lie outside the key of any given passage no longer stand apart polytonally as a separate, superimposed key. They are fused somehow into the prevailing texture. More subtle and less conventional than straight polytonality, this new harmonic style is crystallized in the Variations and reaches still higher stages of consolidation and refinement in the *Short Symphony* and *Statements.*

Copland's harmonies of that entire decade, whether derived through polytonal means or through the more imaginative interpolations upon the diatonic substructure, often ran high in dissonance content. It was thus that he stood as a "modernist" and wild experimentalist to more than just the most conservative part of the public and press (see above, p. 23 ff.). The *avant-gardistes,* on the other hand, exposing his methods to analysis, were aware of the clearly tonal principle to which his "unruly" note-patterns were subordinated. In their eyes Copland was, ironically enough, even in those years a reactionary.

The degree in which diatonic order exerts itself on the variously chromatic, dissonant elements is perhaps best illustrated by the way in which bold, unalloyed triads enter into the Variations at one point without the least anachronism or inconsistency:

Against the prevailingly acid texture of the work, they stand out in startlingly bold relief. The shock and surprise, provoked in the most masterful way, are as powerful as they would be if these triads were crashing cacophonies among cool Mozartean harmonies.

In the hands of a less skilled composer, they might easily strike the ears crudely, appearing in a work otherwise so dissonant. But it is not skill alone that makes them so convincing here. It is also because all through the Variations the play of tones has been governed by the principle of the triad, and however intricate and biting the superimposed non-diatonic elements may be, they originate in diatonic relations—diatonic relations raised to the second power, so to speak (e.g., the major-minor and the ambiguities of secondary key centers).

Instances of passages that are unconditionally diatonic, and much simpler even than the above, are to be found from time to time all through Copland's music from 1925 to 1935. Such passages often are diatonic to the merest auxiliary note, e.g., the close three-part canon of trumpets in the Piano Concerto and the fifteen measures of F major (with subsidiary flavor of A-Phrygian) in the Lento of the *Short Symphony*. Nor did the fact that he abandoned key signatures around 1925 prevent the diatonic principle from dominating. Atonal music, or even chromatic music, was farthest from his mind when he adopted this course. True, the start of the first movement and the close of the last were not, as tradition dictates, always in the same key. But each movement in itself observed a central tone, and the pivotal points of separate movements stood in a planned relation to one another. The abandonment of key signature was merely a means for facilitating an intricate telescoping of a variety of interpolated non-diatonic elements.

Copland's development around 1935, then, was not so arbitrary as it might seem, coming after the *Short Symphony* and *Statements*. But this is the least that may be said for it, and some pains to advance this argument have been taken above merely to tighten up the evolutionary picture. Much more important is the consideration that this style is by no means a sign of retrogression. Copland had not simply levelled off the dissonant elaborations so that the simpler relations beneath might exert their appeal upon a wider public directly and unencumbered. A wider public had been one of his aims. But in the metamorphosis of his harmonic idiom he had also been guided, whether consciously or otherwise, by one of the most vital and inevitable forces of our time. If Copland veered, from 1935 on, more closely to a diatonic path (reaching its apex in *Appalachian Spring*), it is because in that direction these days lie some of the greatest possibilities for discovery. The extraordinary progress in chord-formation from Chopin and Schumann to Strauss and Debussy fastened itself upon a progress in the direction of ever more chromatic harmonies. But what if these advances in chord-formation were to be applied to diatonic harmonies as well? Imagine the vast new areas that would be opened by this means!

Radical musical theorists insist that the only new direction for music is atonality or the replacement of tones by percussion. How wrong they are. For oddly enough, as Copland's textures became more and more diatonic, his sonorities grew fresher and more imaginative—indicating a fallacy in the thinking of our so-called most "advanced" creative minds. Infinite new combinations are available through free association of the seven tones of any mode; through superposition of tones borrowed from another key on a basically diatonic chord; through new doublings within traditional harmonies; and especially through wide vertical spacing, often resulting from ingenious omission of "essential" chord tones that would have been present in older music. In Copland's music and other music of the 'twenties the clash of closely assembled dissonances had often been contrived to produce one recurrent effect: a jarring, percussive sound (Ex. 25A). But the new methods have yielded subtle gradations of beauty.

The matter of chord spacing may possibly turn out to be one of the great musical contributions of the last few decades, and Copland stands close to Stravinsky among those who are most responsible for it. The capacity was developed already in the Variations (Ex. 25B), through chords in which some tones were not directly part of the diatonic series. Subsequently purely diatonic combinations began to appear with greater and greater frequency—their clean texture given new brilliance (Ex. 25C). As in the revelational E-minor chord opening Stravinsky's *Symphonie de Psaumes* (Ex. 25D), new ways of presenting old triads lead to unanticipated qualities (Ex. 25E). Other composers, who must produce a big sound at almost every moment to satisfy their compulsions, cannot avail themselves of the refined and varied beauty that results from an extraordinary gift, such as Copland's, for sparing tones. It is only through this gift that the spaces in the pitch continuum may be presented for their own wonderful luminousness.

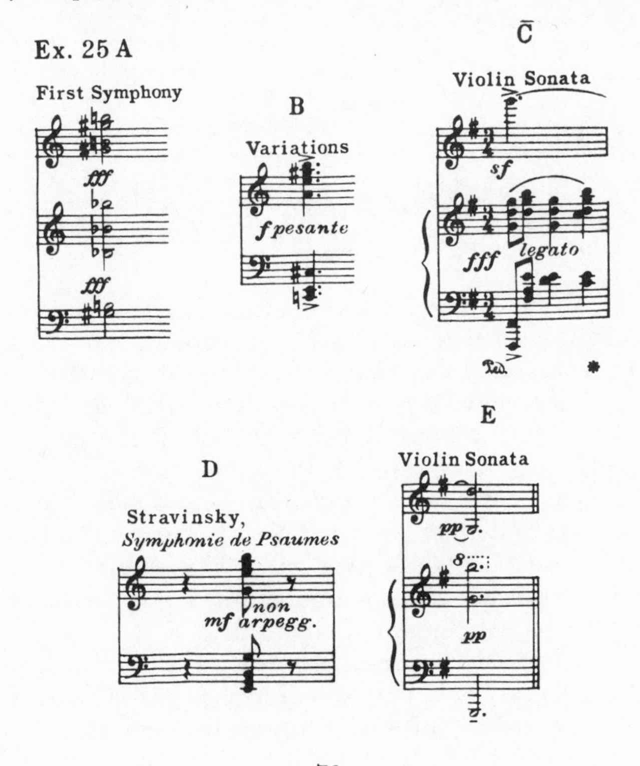

## The Third Symphony

Just how much Copland has achieved in the vertical spread of his notes may be estimated from the spacious qualities of his Third Symphony. Such a passage as the following from the third movement is merely one of many in which a sense of vast expanse is conveyed by the fewest possible notes:

Ex. 26

If, as someone once said, a symphony is "the history of a man", a work of such broad proportions, embodying the various levels of experience that have become part of Copland's conscious and unconscious thought, would inevitably present a kind of panorama of all the musical resources that have through the years formed his musical language. We have already seen how popular material, both jazz and what we more usually know as folk music, conditioned Copland's style even where specific quotation or reference was not the aim. In his Third Symphony we have a summary of almost all of this.

As if in deliberate reaction against the preoccupation in his orchestral works of over a decade, Copland insisted that no extra-musical ideologies were connected with the conception or execution of his symphony, and that nowhere in it will we find direct quotations of the folksong that had seemed appropriate to the scenarios of his ballets and movies and the literary subject matter of other works. It thus must be stressed that the indigenous aspects I shall indicate in it are the more elusive kind to be found in a Haydn symphony with its evocation of Croatian folklore or stately court minuets, rather than the specific kind that exists in Rimsky-Korsakoff's *Russian Easter Overture* or Stravinsky's *Petrouchka.*

It is important that this be understood, because some people are under the impression that Copland has abandoned his more serious musical thinking for folk potpourris. Nothing is farther from the truth, even where *Rodeo* and *Billy the Kid* are concerned. It is understandable enough that these people should be under such a misapprehension, since what they hear most often is *Lincoln Portrait* or *El Salón México*—works that, despite their admirable features, have frankly circumscribed aims. But Copland has, since his conversion in the middle 'thirties, written two substantial sonatas and the Piano Quartet, and to this line of works in abstract forms, paralleling in another dimension his theatrical and other occasional works, the Third Symphony belongs.

Because the Third Symphony was his first orchestral work without extra-musical affiliations since 1934, it naturally was looked forward to as an event of consequence in Copland's career, and the burden on himself to write music of a certain seriousness and to avoid the kind of concrete subject matter of his orchestral works immediately preceding was great indeed. But precisely because the composer did not force himself to say any one thing in the Third Symphony, he seems to be saying very many, though these would be extremely difficult to pin down. For the ways of the unconscious are such that we often express feelings without being aware of them, and these may represent a deeper level of our being when conscious layers are not active to simplify and (as in program music or music otherwise connected with a literary concept) narrow down the sphere of reference.

Among the many things this symphony seems to evoke, its general character of a glorified and expansive hymn—of prayer, of praise, of sorrow, of patriotic sentiment—is what I find most striking. Having dealt with New England and Quaker hymnody, and having sung, more generally, the eulogies of his country and its founders, he does not surprise us when he opens his symphony with a predominantly slow first movement based on three subjects (Ex. 27A, B, and C) in that declamatory style that preserves a

Ex. 27 A

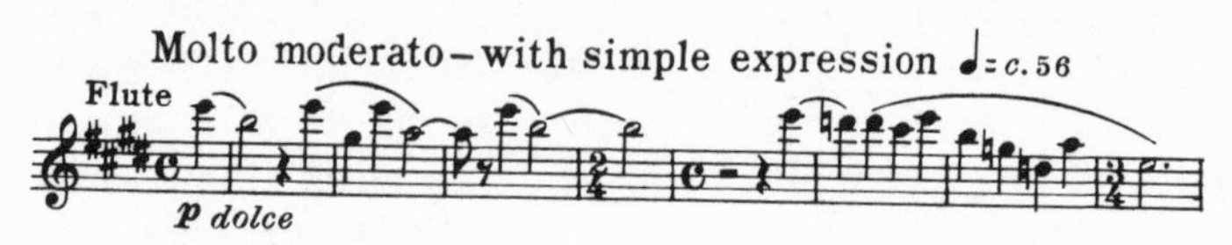


B

C

D

certain essence of the hymn at the same time that it is so thoroughly Copland; or when he opens the fourth movement with a phrase (Ex. 27D) borrowed from his *Fanfare for the Common Man* (composed in 1942 for Eugene Goossens for a series of wartime fanfares), harmonized in block fashion in sixths like a chorale.

Among secondary expressive elements in the symphony, within the fast sections that punctuate the predominantly sustained music, we find remote suggestions of a leisurely, carefree cowboy tune (Ex. 28A), and unleashed Latin American rhythm (Ex. 28B). Evocations of both sources had appeared individually in his separate ventures into the realms of the colloquial during previous years.

Copland's characteristic economy, legitimately sacrificed at times in the past to the demands of a ballet or movie score, seems to have been set aside for the occasion of this symphony as if to answer rather deliberately those critics who have found his style not "big" enough according to the standards established by post-Romantic music. His Third Symphony falls into the broadly rhetorical pattern established for the form from Beethoven and Schumann through Mahler and adorned in our time by Shostakovitch with a special fillip to mass appeal. The slow, broad, Mahleresque first-movement form of Shostakovitch had already been adopted by Roy Harris in his highly inspired, if uneven, symphonies, but this had been converted into thoroughly American terms by recourse to American hymnody. In this respect, though the two are very different, the opening of Copland's Third Symphony shares something with that of Harris's Third Symphony. This is not a case necessarily where influences are involved, for by the time Copland wrote his work the hymnal style for the opening of a symphony had been thoroughly crystallized as a convention in American music, a device that was common property. It was something that existed before Harris had attempted the symphonic form, and it had nothing to do with Shostakovitch, moreover, when it first appeared. We find it in the opening, and most authentic, section of the Ives Third Symphony, which dates back to 1911, and it is strikingly exploited in the *Symphony on a Hymn Tune* of Virgil Thomson, written in 1926.

Along with grandness of conception, the broad symphonic pattern, as it has survived in this century, brings certain features of grandiloquence and flashiness. We observe them in the way rather obvious sentiments are driven at times and forced on audience attention by over-repetition. There is, for example, Copland's protracted sequential development of the motif in Ex. 27c, or the brassy insistence on the last half of the fanfare—recalling both in the motif itself and in its extension Tchaikovsky's all too familiar methods:

This Tchaikovskian motif has become further hackneyed by the recent twist Shostakovitch gave it in the Nazi invasion episode of his *Leningrad Symphony,* and one cannot help feeling satiated with it when it appears again in Copland's symphony, especially since it is taken up so much of the time by the brass. For an explanation of such a lapse in Copland's usually reliable taste it is hard to know where to look. Might it be the frustrations connected with his *Short Symphony?* Was it, perhaps, that this time he wanted his symphony performed? Some share of deference to the current vogue established by successful symphonists and encouraged by conductors and audiences might have been called for.

But let us pardon him for the more blatant measures and be grateful for the many things that are fresh and beautiful in this symphony and that constitute a fruitful direction for him. In place of the short forms or longer works with short episodes prescribed by his previous commissions, the Third Symphony is a work of four highly sustained, sizable movements. The expansive, uninhibited racing of the strings over wide areas of pitch is also a gratifying new element in Copland's music. This device began to manifest itself in the Violin Sonata, its last movement in particular, where an almost classical continuity is achieved. The short phrases that pause, and start up again with accretions, have been developed in a very personal way by Copland, and there is no reason why he should abandon them. But longer lines, spinning themselves out, bring a much needed element of contrast, and the melodic line in the Violin Sonata (Ex. 30A) that constantly progresses to a newer and newer goal over a gently moving accompaniment of gradually changing harmonies is welcome indeed as an alternate mode of proceeding. There is a rapid sequence of dovetailed elements with interesting divagations. It is as if Copland, who had often hugged the ground in the manner of the "modern school" of American dancers, suddenly took flight like a ballet dancer.

In the symphony, the undulating lines are, at moments, still more adventurous—the passage following the slow introduction of the fourth movement, for example. In these days of the ubiquitous abruptly arrested melodic patterns and the phrases that often bog down as soon as they take off, the inspired length of continuously bustling sixteenth notes (extension of the pattern in Ex. 30B)—over two minutes before we come to the first caesura—is rare indeed. Strings zoom up and down, dancing giddily on the heights, and occasionally the spacing between the lines is so wide that it seems to pit aerial stunts against restrained activity on the ground (Ex. 30C). The lovely flute theme from the third movement (Ex. 30D) is the subject of another development that also stands apart for its soaring quality, though the flight here is more gentle, with gracious melodic curves and balletic sighs (30E).

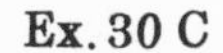

D

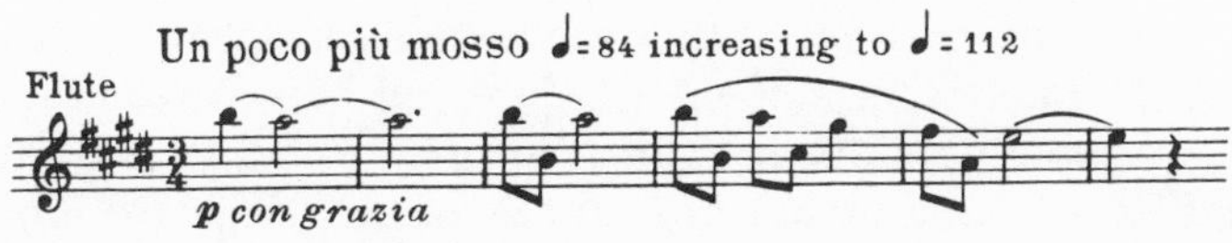


E

In addition to summarizing, in idealized form, the many types of subject matter Copland converted into his own expert terms in the course of the preceding decades, the Third Symphony reflects his enormous progress in orchestration during the period separating the First Symphony from *Appalachian Spring*. Wide vertical spacing of contrapuntal lines or harmonies contributes immeasurably to the lustre and freshness of orchestral sonority, and it thus may be considered that we have already dealt somewhat with the quality of his instrumentation.

In addition to his spacing there are such touches as the delicate use of the celesta in the second movement as background for the theme in Ex. 28A, or, earlier in the movement, the xylophone in the introductory passages (No. 22 in the orchestral score). In both instances he succeeds eminently in avoiding the vulgarity or cuteness often associated with these instruments. He does not hesitate, moreover, to confine long passages to the woodwinds (as at No. 118), so that the effectiveness of the whole string body or the tutti, when called upon, is that much the greater. Mastery of the orchestra is, as a matter of fact, one of the things this symphony indicates very noticeably.

It would seem, then, that the virtues in the symphony go far to extenuate for the few, if obvious, shortcomings. At the same time, let us observe that Copland, keen self-critic that he is, took to heart the most reliable comments and came round, in at least one instance, to the realization that there was some justice in the criticism leveled against the work on the basis of its occasional over-insistence on its material. Thus, in response to a fairly general feeling that the end was unduly extended, he cut eight measures from No. 129 to No. 130 and also the fifth and sixth measures after No. 130. (These rehearsal numbers refer to the first, that is, the present, edition.) Copland was not in the habit of doing anything like this after publication of a work. Like the rest of us he was, however, both surprised and happy to find that even so slight an incision made a difference when the new version was heard in the summer of 1952 at the Berkshire Festival, Bernstein conducting.[1]

---

[1] For a movement by movement analysis of the Third Symphony see my contribution to the Aaron Copland Number of *Tempo*, Autumn 1948, pp. 17–20.

## Period of Consolidation

In the years following the Third Symphony Copland gave more and more evidence of his determination to consolidate his most important achievements. Even so unpretentious a work as the Clarinet Concerto of 1948 is deceptive in its simplicity. Written for Benny Goodman, it inevitably exploits the "hot" jazz improvisation for which that clarinetist is noted. But the very episodes that evoke the sharp-edged, controlled, motoric style of Goodman's brilliant old sextet are often the ones recalling most strongly the stark, dissonant devices that gave Copland the reputation for being an esoteric in the early 'thirties. Observe how much there is in common between Ex. 31A from the Clarinet Concerto and Ex. 31B from the *Short Symphony* of 1933. Both demonstrate Copland's rare skill for achieving a striking effect with the fewest possible notes contained within an incisive rhythmic pattern.

The jazz elements make their entrance into the Concerto in the course of an extended cadenza that connects the two movements and they dominate the fast, second part of the work. The tender first movement is of lyrical cast, with the grace of ballet and the general mood of a slow dance. It was not at all surprising that a work with a first movement of this character and a second movement evocative of jazz should have established itself by 1951 (shortly after its concert and radio premieres) in ballet repertory as musical underpinning for *The Pied Piper* of Jerome Robbins. Yet, with all its readily assimilable exterior and the unproblematic dance content that render it serviceable to the theater, the slow section, like the jazzy part, has its subtleties, too. These are contained largely in the instrumentation, which is confined to strings, harp and piano. From a piano reduction of this score one would never suspect the luminosity that is imparted to the string sonority by the delicate edging of figures in the harp.

The tendency on the part of the most serious music lovers to underestimate the Clarinet Concerto, their failure to appreciate the genuineness of its inspirations, is regrettable, and the clownish excesses of the Robbins choreography have been no help in illuminating the weightiest properties of the score. By contrast, the next work to which Copland gave comparable time and effort has done more, perhaps, than any of his recent music to regain the confidence of those who had rallied around his *Short Symphony* and Piano Variations. I refer to the song cycle, Twelve Poems of Emily Dickinson, completed early in 1950.

The name of Mahler has come up more than once above in allusions to Copland's Third Symphony. The Viennese master seems also to have had something to do with the conception of the Dickinson songs. It is a different side of Mahler, a more sympathetic side, that suggests itself here—the wistfulness that characterizes his condensed song forms rather than the rhetoric of the distended symphonies. Even if Mahler had not meant so much to Copland previously, the sheer challenge of setting poems so preoccupied with death as those of Dickinson would have been enough to establish an affinity with the composer of *Kindertotenlieder*.

The kinship to that composer manifested in the Dickinson songs is intangible, indeed, a mere aroma that the average Mahler enthusiast might easily miss if his experience with contemporary music and Copland's individual style, in particular, is limited. In fact, the wide, jagged skips of Copland's vocal line might easily infuriate your Mahler enthusiast just as they infuriated a few conservative critics and voice "experts". But it was precisely the strength, the boldness of these devices that delighted the rest of us (Ex. 32). The quality of the inspirations in the Dickinson settings, within an idiom that does not give its secret up too freely, places them in the category of the finest contemporary song literature. The cycle brings Copland's purest melodic contours (the interval of the third again) into association with the vocal procedures that have become pretty much the property of the advanced chromatic schools in existence since Schoenberg came on the scene.

Ex. 32
Sleep is supposed to be.

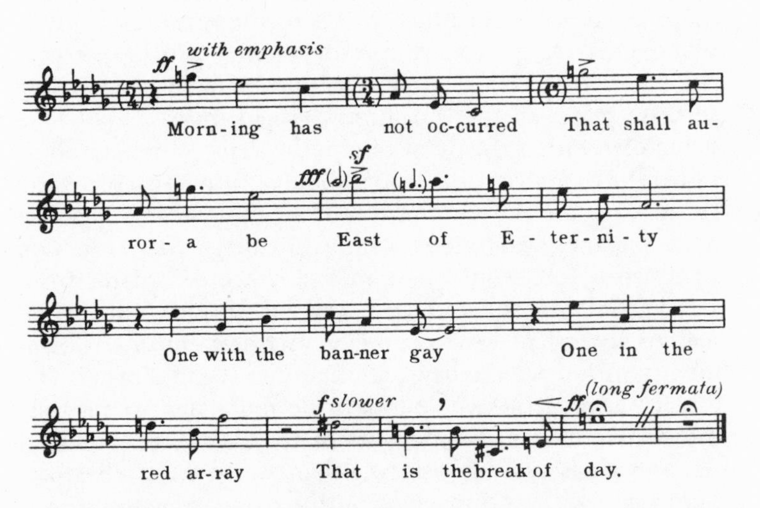


With his next important work, the Quartet for Piano and Strings (1950), Copland seemed even more emphatically to be seeking some rapprochement with the movement promulgated by Schoenberg and developed by his Viennese disciples, Berg and Webern. In this respect it is tempting to conclude that Copland was merely reflecting a general tendency toward reconciliation of two camps that had formerly been considered irreconcilable—that is to say, between the chromaticists, among whom Schoenberg is generally regarded to be the key figure, and the faithful diatonicists for whom Stravinsky is the master. As twelve-tone music, and especially the compromises Berg wrought with it, became more widely accepted among enlightened concert-goers (though still not among the general public), composers who did not subscribe particularly to the system began to recognize the benefits to be derived from encompassing some of its devices without becoming partisan. This is what Copland seems to have done in the Piano Quartet, for it would be gross simplification to say he had adopted partisanship among Schoenberg's disciples merely by using a "tone-row".

Copland had already explored possibilities of a "tone-row," as we have observed, in his Piano Variations, back in 1930, though very much in his own terms. Thus, in his Piano Quartet he was simply developing further certain principles of serial treatment with which he had already come to grips. In the Variations he had investigated these principles with a theme of obvious C-sharp minor implications. Now he ventures more boldly into the chromatic realm with an eleven-tone row (Ex. 33A). There is precedent for an eleven-tone row in Schoenberg's Serenade, Op. 24. Such a row would not, in itself, keep Copland from strict serial procedure. But it was not his aim, nor did he seek in any other way to emulate Viennese chromatic complexity. The personality and manner are his own. The theme suggests the whole-tone scale more than it suggests the elusive chromatic contours of typical twelve-tone music, and he is more concerned than the strict twelve-tone composers with the motives outlined by segments of the theme. Thus, in the fast middle movement much is made of the opening three notes, with the first of them transposed to the octave below (Ex. 33B). The abruptly clipped phrase that results, and the excitement it engenders are typically Coplandesque. Absorption of a few serial procedures merely serves to invigorate his own style and open up new channels for development.

It will be observed in Ex. 33A that after eleven different tones are stated the opening B-flat returns, and the first and last tones, identical except for range, act as a frame for the theme. Starting with the final B-flat, and proceeding in retrograde, the composer derives a tender little segment later on. The first part of the theme is, however, a bit too elementary in rhythm and too evocative of the whole-tone scale to lend itself happily to quite so much prominence as Copland gives it in the course of the first and last movements. It is obviously amenable to the declamatory, hymnic style in which Copland has long shown himself at home, and it fails to bring in its wake either the most novel or the most inspired ideas of the work.

## Copland and Hollywood

During the days when Copland was seriously involved writing his Third Symphony, the characteristic pull in the other direction did not cease to exert itself and he found time to write the music for a documentary film, *The Cummington Story*. His first and only other documentary had been *The City,* and it had been the success of this score in its context that had attracted the attention of Hollywood and led to his years of affluence as a composer for commercial films at intervals from 1939 to 1949.

Copland's arrival in Hollywood marked something of a milestone there for, while in Europe it is altogether customary for the top composers to write movie scores, in America men who specialize in this medium, and are little known outside of it, are usually intrusted with the task. There are, of course, exceptions, like Louis Gruenberg, who arrived in Hollywood with a reputation already established, but it is a long time since anything has been heard from him except through the sound-track. George Antheil is another who has settled in Hollywood, but his movie scores have not been representative of his finest musical effort, and he has not, it seems to me, produced anything comparable to Gruenberg's music for *The Commandos Strike at Dawn*. And there have been, in addition, visitors like Bernard Herrmann from time to time, to contribute distinguished scores.[1]

But a composer of Copland's magnitude, maintaining in Hollywood the same high standards that he would maintain anywhere else, was another matter. When he undertakes a movie score, Copland, after studying the cue-sheet, with its timing and description of sequences, and after seeing the film a few times, does not, as is customary, write his music without any further reference to the screen. On the contrary, he sees the film again and again while writing. In an informative discussion of his method, Otis L. Guernsey, Jr., pointed out that he "works in constant association with the film. He will sit down with individual scenes, running them over and over, and they induce musical ideas in him the way an electrified coil induces magnetism in an iron bar."[2] This method of working so close to the film in order to extract its own essence, rather than impose music upon it, immediately distinguished him among

[1] Virgil Thomson's Pulitzer Prize-winning music for *Louisiana Story* was not for a Hollywood film but for an independent project.

[2] Sunday drama section, New York Herald Tribune, Sept. 4, 1949.

movie-score writers and helped raise the standards of Hollywood music in general. Echoes of his style were soon to be heard in the music of other score-writers and his idiom became a mark of prestige. David Raksin and Hugo Friedhofer in particular made his style their own, but in doing so underlined Copland's superiority in shaping the music to the dramatic requirements, the mood and local color. Thus Friedhofer's score to *The Best Years of Our Lives,* which is very derivative, curiously hooks an idiom evolved by Copland for the chaste New England scenes of *Our Town* onto the very different atmosphere of readjustment of veterans in the Midwest.

Copland is very careful, on the contrary, about the appropriateness of the music to the *mise-en-scène,* and in some cases he becomes quite fastidious in this regard. "I don't like to hear a piano in the music for an outdoor scene", he is quoted as having remarked. "You can stretch the imagination for other instruments, but a piano is such an indoor thing—you can't run along with it or carry it from place to place. I may be the only one who feels this way, but I just cannot connect a piano with the outdoors."[1]

It is, of course, a good thing for Hollywood composers to lean on Copland as a relief from the inevitable Delius, Strauss, Tchaikovsky that serve as their sources. And it is also good to see other composers taking more care since Copland's advent. But there is still one very important respect in which Copland has an advantage over most of the others. For he has refused to yield to the assembly-line method of the majority of Hollywood composers, who have separate orchestrators come in and recast things their own way after the score-writer has done his job. Copland orchestrates his own music. In general his accomplishment has been to simplify Hollywood music and to give it, even where folksong is not quoted, an American flavor.

Virgil Thomson considers Copland's score for *The Red Pony* "the most elegant . . . yet composed and executed

[1] *Ibid.*

under 'industry conditions', as Hollywood nowadays calls itself . . . Mr. Copland himself, Hollywood's most accomplished composer, has not in his earlier films—*Of Mice and Men, North Star* and *Our Town*—produced for cinematic drama a musical background so neatly cut and fitted."[1] I agree with Mr. Thomson as to the "perfection of the musical tailoring in this picture", but there are many set pieces such as the threshing-machine episode in *Of Mice and Men* and the funeral procession on the hill in *Our Town* that are decidedly on a higher plane—effective both with the picture and as excerpts—than any one sequence from *The Red Pony.* The fact that the two earlier films were far superior in quality is a great help too, for the association of the music with inferior cinematic material is injurious to the effect it has on us.

True, Copland has remarked that he "never writes music for something he doesn't like". But while a film is still in the script stage it is not always easy to anticipate the value of the outcome and I believe that even Copland would agree that though he was fascinated by the idea of *The Red Pony* the end-product was not all that it could have been. Copland was, of course, a natural choice for a Western film and the sequence of Tom's fight with the buzzards over the body of the dead pony is underpinned with violent measures that are enormously effective:

[1]Sunday music page, New York Herald Tribune, April 10, 1949.

The concert excerpts from *The Red Pony* form a sort of children's suite that harks back to *The Second Hurricane.*

Deterioration in the quality of the films Copland worked on started with *North Star* and corresponded with the general deterioration in Hollywood that set in during the 'forties. But Copland's own skill increased. The chamber-music character of some of the music for *Of Mice and Men* had been very welcome indeed as a relief from the elephantine orchestra that is Hollywood's convention. But not until later did Copland exploit the possibilities of montage the sound-track affords. In *The Heiress* he used the "trick", as he frankly calls it, of having a string orchestra and the regular studio orchestra separately record the same music and then superimposing them. The added strings, duplicating the winds and the original strings, gave increased expressivity for the intense moment when the heroine breaks down at the end, while her rejected, money-seeking suitor is banging on the bolted door.[1]

*The Heiress,* though a better picture than *The Red Pony,* gave him less opportunity for music of vitality and scope. Someone has remarked that this is because it is an "indoor" picture, and Copland is better disposed towards outdoor scenes. But I think it may be that the stagey adaptation is too even-tempered, and for long stretches a dance band plays *Plaisir d'amour.* Copland discreetly alludes to this tune later on in a distinctly Coplandesque way. The producers wanted him, in addition, to make a bald, literal statement of it for the signature music at the opening of the film. But Copland refused to descend to this level, and a Hollywood score-writer was called in to do so. As a result, not only the realistic dance sequence, but also the music for the first minute of the film, underpinning the initial credits, is not from his pen. It is only when his name

[1] The process is known in Hollywood as "sweetening". In an article on movie music in the New York Times magazine section, Nov. 6, 1949, p. 28 ff., Copland credits Miklos Rosza and Bernard Herrmann for comparable tricks; he also, in this article, deals with the problems in general confronting a composer in Hollywood.

appears on the screen among the later credits that the taut, luminous Copland sounds simultaneously make their initial and unmistakable appearance.

There are some who look askance on the idea of a serious musician writing for Hollywood. This is enough to assure them that a composer's integrity is not to be trusted in anything he does. The notion is thoroughly unreasonable when we consider that composers do all sorts of things to support themselves, including teaching and writing books or musical criticism, and even if we disregarded entirely Copland's Hollywood activity as merely an accessory means such as these, he would still rate high among contemporary composers on the basis of his other accomplishments. Many portions of his movie music not only serve their function admirably, but also stand up excellently in the concert hall. It is a delight to hear them in the *Our Town Suite* and *Music for Movies.*

## Copland's Americanism and Influence

For its indigenous aspects alone, Copland's music must remain an achievement of American culture. This aspect, as we have seen, was well developed even before he had recourse to folksong. Doubtless his jazz period was a step in this direction but Gershwin, too, had used jazz, had used it with inspiration. Yet Gershwin's works had been weighted down by symphonic interludes of European tone-poems, poorly integrated. Copland, with more craft, imagination, constructive power, molded the foundations of his style partly out of the same elements that made up jazz itself. When specific allusions to the popular form were removed or sublimated after 1928, there remained the framework which had been partly determined by jazz as one of the sources of his Americanism. Almost everything about his music of this second period was obscure to most people, but a critic with Rosenfeld's perceptions could find an essence in common with that of the Empire State Building.

When New England and Shaker hymnody and cowboy

songs were later incorporated, an indigenous substratum had thus already been well developed. In tapping this store of raw material, Copland was no doubt spurred on by the additional earmarks of Americanism that would come in its wake. In those years he was very much concerned over the foreign market, South America in particular, and he spoke of the need for some local stamp so that our music would be recognizable there.

But folk music had an important attraction for him of another sort. There were the plastic possibilities of the material itself, and in this respect a Portuguese tune for the chorus, *Las Agachadas,* completed in 1942, or the Mexican tune in *El Salón México* fulfilled the same function for him as *Goodbye, Old Paint* in *Billy the Kid.* The parallel of Stravinsky suggests itself, who borrowed Pergolesi's tunes for *Pulcinella* with the same interest in their possibilities as when he borrowed his native folk tunes for *Petrouchka.*

It is interesting, too, in this regard, that Copland had quoted in his *Short Symphony* a German tune he had heard in a German film, *Congress Dances (Der Kongress Tanzt),* around the time this work was composed:

Ex. 35

Precise and rhythmic ♩= 144

ff

He was not trying to make any specific reference; he was merely fascinated by the notes. The fact that it is a quotation has nothing but clinical or historical importance.

Whether the compiled material is American or otherwise, once it is incorporated into Copland's music, the problem is its conversion into his own terms, with or without evocation of the source. As I have already indicated, a predisposition existed towards certain folksongs and not towards others, and this was important in governing his choice. Traditional tunes provided extra materials to work with, but the materials themselves were merely so many different specific manifestations of qualities that had already been present in his music. I take it to be significant that before *Billy the Kid* and *Rodeo* were even conceived, his *Music for Radio,* in a Columbia Broadcasting System contest for a more descriptive title, brought forth as the winning suggestion *Saga of the Prairies.* Earlier than this, the Lento of the *Short Symphony* had the spaciousness that has been associated by some people, when it has reappeared in his more recent works, with the vastness of the American landscape.

If, for example, a thoroughgoing New Yorker has been capable of distilling from cowboy tunes the intense solitude and aridness of our immense and unpopulated plains (as an English critic, W. H. Mellers, has observed),[1] it is, I think, because he can grasp that these sentiments are really not so far from the solitude and aridness he himself has experienced in the completely antithetical setting of his own city streets, where the sense of isolation may be all the greater because it is felt in the midst of hundreds of people passing by.

Those who consider the achievement of an indigenous style prerequisite to America's proverbial "coming of age" should notice the way Copland has embodied this acute awareness of his own immediate environment while evincing, at the same time, a genuine curiosity to explore the widest reaches of his surroundings from New England (*Our Town*) to Spanish America (*Danzón Cubano* and *El Salón México*). And he has found the means of idealizing American folk tunes in their own terms and in terms of his own native experience—unlike a preceding generation that glibly couched them in the most stereotyped European molds. Yet the value of his accomplishment rests on some-

---

[1] W. H. Mellers, *American Music,* in *Kenyon Review,* Summer 1943.

thing more than merely this. Whether confronted with the tunes of his own country or of its southern neighbors, his primary concern appears to have been how much beauty and substance could be achieved by their adoption and manipulation.

However deliberate Copland may have been in embracing his native folk sources (including jazz) to develop a native style, it is altogether normal for one to take advantage of the beauty given or even potential in the qualities immediately surrounding one. Thus, if it was the same objectivity that had turned him originally to South American subject matter and that of the United States, it was the latter that understandably prevailed in the end in the shaping of his basic style, because it was nearer home.

Charles Ives and Virgil Thomson had preceded Copland in the exploration of American folk material, and Ernst Bacon and Jerome Moross are among recent explorers of this field. Since Copland has pursued the matter further than any of the others he has done the most to illuminate for many of us the popular musical heritage of our country. It might even be said, with a certain irony, to be sure, that Copland has had more influence on American folk music than it has had on him. For he has added to our knowledge of certain of its areas merely by dissemination, through his music, of the choicest tunes. Moreover, the astonishing number of young men who have, in the use of folk music, come under his influence did so, perhaps, because they found an Americanism that was in a way more valid than what they could acquire by having recourse to jazz or folk music directly.

There are many ways of handling folk material, and the four composers I have mentioned have all distinguished themselves in the process through expert methods that are mutually distinct and distinct from Copland's. But most of the younger men who have taken up the cause (for example, Elie Siegmeister, Gail Kubik, and, in his early works, Leo Smit) dress up the colloquialisms with much the same trappings as Copland does—his characteristic harmony, cumulative phrase-extension, and declamation.

These methods are, to start with, so well crystallized in Copland's music—at times even unduly formularized—that it is doubtful they have within them the potentiality for so much further exploitation. Moreover, many of them are so personal that they are transferable only when extreme caution is exerted.

The phenomenon has occurred before in music—for example, the aftermath of Wagner or Debussy. Each of these masters had an idiom that was to so great a degree an expression of the self that it was incapable of becoming a sufficiently plastic convention for a subsequent generation to adopt as a solid basis upon which to proceed. True, there was much to learn from Wagner's handling of mass effects or from Debussy's sensitive chord-spacing, which was one of the chief things contributing to the later harmonic innovations of Copland and Stravinsky. But the idioms of Wagner and Debussy, regarded in more specific terms, were pretty nearly exhausted by these composers themselves. Similarly, Schoenberg has liberated modern music, but his system was so thoroughly exploited by Webern that its further exploration presents a grave challenge.

The era of Mozart was different in this regard, offering a universal language capable of further exploitation in its broadest features. And in our time, Stravinsky, since 1923, has restored this type of universality. It is interesting, however, that in our country the most gifted young men who have, for this reason, taken Stravinsky as their guide, have also preserved an allegiance to Copland, limiting themselves to certain important lessons his music offers rather than adopting his style as a whole. Irving Fine, Alexei Haieff, and Harold Shapero belong to this group, and they are not only indebted to Copland for his clarification of the musical medium, but occasionally even evoke his specific formulas and melodic curves in passing.[1]

---

[1] See Shapero's Sonata for piano, four hands, the theme of the Variations in Fine's Music for Piano, and parts of Haieff's Five Piano Pieces.

The musical scene, viewed more generally, discloses that there is scarcely any young American composer who has not, at one point or another, reflected the powerful beam Copland has cast (except, of course, those who are protected behind the armor of atonality). They range from Leonard Bernstein, who reflects it very powerfully, to men like Lukas Foss and Norman Dello Joio, who reflect it at certain moments only and at a distance. Influences, however inevitable they are, have always been fraught with dangers, and there may still be a bona fide Copland disciple who will come along with the mechanism to divert them into significantly new channels.

The extent of Copland's influence is, however, apart from anything else, an indication of his forcefulness as a creative artist. The fact that his own devices appear so formularized when adopted as currency in the general musical market is of far less consequence. What remains the problem in Copland's case—and this matter, already referred to above, needs re-emphasis in closing—is the belittling effect the Copland of *Lincoln Portrait* has, for some listeners, on the Copland of the Sextet. This is because contemporary esthetic theory is inevitably becoming involved in half-truths. There is a constant bifurcation of concepts with the result that doing one thing is often taken as excluding another. Many insist that music achieves its loftiest aims by suppressing form and concentrating on feeling. Within the category of feeling it is further insisted that only the loftiest feelings are admissible into the loftiest music. Or there are those who deny feeling; and those, like Satie, who, understandably fed up with the 19th-century *"sérieux à tout prix"*—to borrow Milhaud's phrase—lean towards the other extreme of music with only the thinnest or mildest feeling content. At such a time it is no surprise that the well-rounded musicianship of Copland and the emotional fullness of his accomplishment may easily be underestimated.

Let us not forget that Copland's trend away from his more austere style of the early 'thirties did not only result in a music for wider audience. It also resulted in a new melodic element that was a valuable factor when he returned to more serious works like the sonatas and the Third Symphony.

The people who know Copland's music of the earlier 'thirties are, alas, all too few. The more recent works, those for a wider audience, much as they fulfill a very important function and gratifying as they are even to more demanding listeners, have unhappily driven his more serious works altogether from orchestra concerts. But those who are fortunate enough to be acquainted with Copland's earlier music are wise enough to look for his earlier ingenuities in his more recent works, while others brusquely assume that any music dealing with material so simple as the folksong inevitably sacrifices any depth of treatment.

It is, to be sure, unfortunate that Copland is known for his most amiable works rather than for his most earnest, uncompromising pieces such as those that were written around 1930 and 1950. But Copland shares with the masters the capacity for turning out his most casual work with the sensitivity and dignity of his most ambitious ones, and this is something to be devoutly thankful for in his music for wider use. Let us be thankful, moreover, for the new seriousness that has made itself felt in his recent Dickinson songs and Piano Quartet, and let us look forward to the day when his subsequent orchestral works encompass it as well.

It is natural for the average listener to delight in music based on folksongs, and to credit the composer for the appeal that these by themselves possess. It is just as natural for the experienced listener—who is justified in a way—to regard one folk adaptation as very much like any other. Copland's case requires a further perception on the part of both.

# APPENDIX

# I. List of Works

| *Title* | *Date of Completion* | *First Performance* | *Publisher* |
|---|---|---|---|
| *Scherzo Humoristique: The Cat and the Mouse* for piano | 1920 | Sept. 1921. Composer, Fontainebleau School | Durand |
| *Old Poem* (Arthur Waley, transl. from Chinese) for voice & pia. | 1920 | Feb. 1922. Charles Hubbard, Société Musicale Indépendante, Paris | Senart |
| *Pastorale* (Edward Powys Mathers, transl. from Kafiristan) for voice & pia. | 1921 | The same | MS |
| Four Motets for chorus of mixed voices *a cappella* | 1921 | Feb. 1937. Cho. con. Nadia Boulanger, Paris | MS |
| Passacaglia for piano | 1922 | Jan. 1923. Daniel Ericourt, Société Musicale Indépendante, Paris | Senart |
| *Grohg*, ballet | 1922-25 | | MS |
| Excerpts: | | | |
| *Cortège Macabre* | 1923 | May 1, 1925. Rochester Sym. Orch. con. Hanson | MS |
| *Dance Symphony* | 1925 | Apr. 15, 1931. Philadelphia Orch. con. Stokowski | Arrow Music Press (Cos Cob Pub.) |
| *As it fell upon a day* (Richard Barnefield) for voice, flute, & clarinet | 1923 | Feb. 6, 1924. Ada MacLeish, Société Musicale Indépendante, Paris | New Music |
| Symphony for Organ and Orchestra | 1924 | Jan. 11, 1925. Boulanger, N. Y. Sym. Orch. con. Damrosch | MS |
| Two Choruses for Women's Voices<br>1. *The House on the Hill* (Edward A. Robinson), *a cappella*<br>2. *An Immorality* (Ezra Pound), pia. acc. | 1925 | Apr. 24, 1925. Women's University Glee Club con. Gerald Reynolds | E. C. Schirmer |

| Title | Date of Completion | First Performance | Publisher |
|---|---|---|---|
| *Music for the Theater* for small orchestra | 1925 | Nov. 20, 1925. Boston Sym. Orch. con. Koussevitzky | Arrow Music Press (Cos Cob Pub.) |
| Two Pieces for violin & piano<br>1. *Nocturne*<br>2. *Ukulele Serenade* | 1926 | Apr. 19, 1926. Samuel Dushkin & Composer, S.M.I., Paris | Schott Söhne |
| Concerto for Piano and Orchestra | 1926 | Jan. 28, 1927. Composer, Boston Sym. Orch. con. Koussevitzky | Arrow Music Press (Cos Cob Pub.) |
| *Two Blues* for piano | 1926 | | |
| 1. *Sentimental Melody* | | 1927. Composer, Ampico recording | Schott Söhne |
| 2. *Blues No. 2*[1] | | May 7, 1942. Hugo Balzo, Montevideo | *Boletin Latino-Americano de Musica,* 1941. *Suplemento Musical* |
| Song (E. E. Cummings) for voice & piano | 1927 | | Arrow Music Press (Cos Cob Pub.) |
| Two Pieces for String Quartet<br>1. Rondino<br>2. Lento Molto | 1923<br>1928 | May 6, 1928. Copland-Sessions Concerts, N. Y. | MS |
| Also arr. for string orchestra | 1928 | Dec. 14, 1928. Boston Sym. Orch. con. Koussevitzky | Arrow Music Press |
| Vocalise for voice & piano | 1928 | New Music Quarterly Recording. Ethel Luening, Composer | Leduc |

[1] The fourth of the *Four Piano Blues,* see p. 112.

| Title | Date of Completion | First Performance | Publisher |
| --- | --- | --- | --- |
| First Symphony (version without organ of Sym. for Organ & Orch.) | 1928 | Jan. 18, 1934. Chicago Sym. Orch. con. Stock (Scherzo first perf. Nov. 4, 1927, Philadelphia Orch. con. Reiner) | Arrow Music Press (Cos Cob Pub.) |
| Also first mov. Prelude arr. for small orch. | 1934 | Feb. 25, 1934. New Chamber Orch. con. B. Herrmann, N. Y. | *Musical Mercury* Magazine |
| *Symphonic Ode* for orchestra | 1928-29 | Feb. 19, 1932. Boston Sym. Orch. con. Koussevitzky | MS |
| *Vitebsk,* Study on a Jewish Theme for violin, 'cello, & piano | 1929 | Feb. 16, 1929. Gieseking, pf; O. Onnou, vn; R. Maas, vcl, League of Composers, N.Y. | Arrow Music Press (Cos Cob Pub.) |
| Piano Variations | 1930 | Jan. 4, 1931. Composer, L. of C., N.Y. | Arrow Music Press (Cos Cob Pub.) |
| *Miracle at Verdun,* incidental music | 1931 | Mar. 1931. Theatre Guild production, N.Y. | MS |
| *Elegies* for violin & viola[1] | 1932 | Apr. 2, 1933. Ivor & Charlotte Karman, L. of C., N.Y. | MS |
| *Short Symphony* | 1932-33 | Nov. 23, 1934. Orquesta Sinfónica de México con. Chávez, Mexico, D.F. | MS |
| *Statements* for orchestra | 1933-34 | Jan. 9, 1936 (2 movements) Minneapolis Sym. Orch. con. Ormandy<br>Jan. 7, 1942 (complete). N.Y. Phil.-Sym. Orch. con. Mitropoulos | Boosey & Hawkes |

[1] Withdrawn.

| Title | Date of Completion | First Performance | Publisher |
|---|---|---|---|
| *Hear Ye! Hear Ye!*, ballet | 1934 | Nov. 30, 1934. Ruth Page & Co., Chicago Opera House, con. Ganz | MS |
| Two Children's Pieces for piano<br>1. *Sunday Afternoon Music*<br>2. *The Young Pioneers* | 1936 | Feb. 24, 1936. Composer, N.Y. | C. Fischer |
| *El Salón México* for orchestra | 1936 | Aug. 27, 1937. Orq. Sinf. de México con. Chávez | Boosey & Hawkes |
| *The Second Hurricane* (Edwin Denby). Play-opera for high-school performance | 1937 | Apr. 21, 1937. Henry St. Music School, N.Y., con. Lehman Engel | C. C. Birchard |
| *Music for Radio (Saga of the Prairies)* for orchestra | 1937 | July 25, 1937. Columbia Broadcasting Sym. con. Barlow | Boosey & Hawkes |
| Sextet (arr. of *Short Symphony*) for string quart., clar., & pia. | 1937 | Feb. 26, 1939. P. Winter, H. Rosoff, E. Vardi, B. Greenhouse, A. Christman, J. Sidorsky, N.Y. | Boosey & Hawkes |
| *Billy the Kid*, ballet | 1938 | Oct. 1938. Eugene Loring & Ballet Caravan, Chicago | Boosey & Hawkes |
| *Outdoor Overture* for orchestra | 1938 | Dec. 16, 1938. High School of Music & Art con. Alex. Richter, N.Y. | Boosey & Hawkes |
| Also arr. for band | 1941 | June 1942. Goldman Band con. Composer, N. Y. | Boosey & Hawkes |
| *Lark* (Genevieve Taggard) for chorus of mixed voices, bar. solo, *a cappella* | 1938 | Apr. 13, 1943. Collegiate Chorale con. Robert Shaw, N.Y. | E. C. Schirmer |
| *The Five Kings*, incidental music | 1939 | Feb. 27, 1939. Mercury Theatre production, Boston | MS |
| *Quiet City*, incidental music for Irwin Shaw's play | 1939 | Apr. 16, 1939. Group Theatre production, N.Y. | MS |

| Title | Date of Completion | First Performance | Publisher |
|---|---|---|---|
| *The City,* music for a documentary film | 1939 | N.Y. World's Fair, 1939 | MS |
| *From Sorcery to Science,* music for a puppet show | 1939 | N.Y. World's Fair, 1939 | MS |
| *Of Mice and Men,* music for a Hal Roach film | 1939 | Spring 1940 | MS |
| *Our Town,* music for a United Artists film | 1940 | Winter 1940 | MS |
| *Our Town,* music from the film score, for orch. (also arr. for piano solo) | 1940 | June 9, 1940. Columbia Broadcasting Sym. con. Barlow | Boosey & Hawkes |
| *John Henry,* Railroad Ballad for small orchestra | 1940 | Mar. 5, 1940. Columbia Broadcasting Sym. con. Barlow | Boosey & Hawkes |
| *Quiet City* for trumpet, Eng. horn, & string orchestra | 1940 | Jan. 28, 1941. Saidenberg Little Sym. con. Daniel Saidenberg, N.Y. | Boosey & Hawkes |
| Piano Sonata | 1941 | Oct. 21, 1941. Composer, Buenos Aires | Boosey & Hawkes |
| *Episode* for organ | 1941 | Mar. 9, 1941. William Strickland, N.Y. | H. W. Gray |
| *Las Agachadas* (The Shake-Down Song) for cho. of mixed voices *a cappella* | 1942 | Mar. 25, 1942. Schola Cantorum con. Hugh Ross, N.Y. | Boosey & Hawkes |
| *Lincoln Portrait* for speaker & orchestra | 1942 | May 14, 1942. Wm. Adams, Cincinnati Sym. Orch. con. Kostelanetz | Boosey & Hawkes |
| *Rodeo,* ballet | 1942 | Oct. 16, 1942. Agnes de Mille, Ballet Russe de Monte Carlo con. Allers, N.Y. | MS |
| *Four Dance Episodes* from *Rodeo* | —— | June 22, 1943. N.Y. Phil.-Sym. Orch. Stadium Concerts con. Smallens | Boosey & Hawkes |

| Title | Date of Completion | First Performance | Publisher |
| --- | --- | --- | --- |
| *Music for Movies,*[1] for small orch. | 1942 | Feb. 17, 1943. Saidenberg Little Sym. con. Saidenberg, N.Y. | MS |
| *Fanfare for the Common Man* for brass & percussion | 1942 | Mar. 14, 1943. Cincinnati Sym. Orch. con. Goossens | Boosey & Hawkes |
| *Danzón Cubano* for 2 pianos (also arr. for orchestra) | 1942 | Dec. 17, 1942. Leonard Bernstein & Composer, League of Composers, N.Y. | Boosey & Hawkes |
| *North Star,* music for a Samuel Goldwyn film | 1943 | Oct. 1943 | MS |
| Sonata for Violin and Piano | 1943 | Jan. 17, 1944. Ruth Posselt & Composer, N.Y. | Boosey & Hawkes |
| *Appalachian Spring,* ballet for 13 instruments (also arr. for sym. orch.) | 1944 | Oct. 30, 1944. Martha Graham & Co. con. Louis Horst, Washington, D.C. | Boosey & Hawkes |
| *Letter from Home* for radio orch. (also arr. for sym. orch.) | 1944 | Oct. 17, 1944. Philco Radio Orch. con. Paul Whiteman | Boosey & Hawkes in prep. |
| *Jubilee Variation,* on a theme by Eugene Goossens, for orch. | 1944 | Apr. 1945. Cincinnati Sym. Orch. con. Goossens | MS |
| *The Cummington Story,* music for a documentary film | 1945 | O.W.I. film | MS |
| Third Symphony | 1946 | Oct. 18, 1946. Boston Sym. Orch. con. Koussevitzky | Boosey & Hawkes |

[1]Comprises *New England Countryside* from *The City; Barley Wagons* from *Of Mice and Men; Sunday Traffic* from *The City; Story of Grovers Corners* from *Our Town;* and *Threshing Machines* from *Of Mice and Men.*

| Title | Date of Completion | First Performance | Publisher |
|---|---|---|---|
| *In the Beginning* (Biblical text) for cho. of mixed voices & mezzo-sopr. solo *a cappella* | 1947 | May 2, 1947. Nell Tangeman, Collegiate Chorale con. Shaw, Cambridge, Mass. | Boosey & Hawkes |
| *Four Piano Blues* | 1948[1] | Mar. 13, 1950. Leo Smit, N.Y. | Boosey & Hawkes |
| *The Red Pony,* music for a Republic film | 1948 | Spring 1948 | MS |
| Suite from *The Red Pony* | 1948 | Nov. 1, 1948. Houston Sym. Orch. con. Kurtz | Boosey & Hawkes |
| Concerto for Clarinet with Strings, Harp, and Piano | 1948 | Nov. 6, 1950. Benny Goodman & NBC Sym. con. Reiner | Boosey & Hawkes |
| *Preamble* for speaker & orchestra | 1949 | Dec. 10, 1949. Laurence Olivier & Boston Sym. Orch. con. Bernstein | Boosey & Hawkes in prep. |
| *The Heiress,* music for a Paramount film | 1949 | Fall 1949 | MS |
| Twelve Poems of Emily Dickinson, song cycle for voice & piano | 1950 | May 18, 1950. Alice Howland & Composer, Columbia Univ. Fest. of Contemporary Music | Boosey & Hawkes |
| Old American Songs, newly arranged for voice & piano | 1950 | June 17, 1950. Peter Pears & Benjamin Britten, Aldeburgh, Eng. | Boosey & Hawkes |
| Quartet for Piano and Strings | 1950 | Oct. 29, 1950. Elizabeth Sprague Coolidge Foundation 25th Anniv. Fest., Washington | Boosey & Hawkes |

[1] No. 1 completed 1947; No. 2, 1934; No. 3, 1948; No. 4, 1926.

## Juvenilia

Capriccio for violin and piano, *c.* 1916
*Moment Musicale:* A Tone Poem for piano, 1917
*Melancholy* (a song à la Debussy) for voice and piano, text by Jeffrey Farnol, 1917
*Danse Charactéristique* for piano, four-hands, *c.* 1917-18
*Waltz Caprice* for piano, 1918
*Night Song* for voice and piano, text by Aaron Schaffer, 1918
*Poème* for 'cello and piano, 1918
*Three Sonnets* for piano, 1918-20
*Simone* for voice and piano, text by Remy de Gourmont, 1919
*Lament* for 'cello and piano (unfinished), *c.* 1919
Prelude No. 1 for violin and piano, 1919
*Music I Heard* for voice and piano, text by Conrad Aiken, 1920
Prelude No. 2 for violin and piano, 1921
*Trois Esquisses (Moods)* for piano:

1. *Amertume,* 1920
2. *Pensif,* 1921
3. *Jazzy,* 1921

Sonata for piano, 1920-21

# II. List of Records

*Works are listed in alphabetical order by title. The year given is the release date of the recording.*

*Appalachian Spring* (Suite from the Ballet)

Boston Symphony Orchestra, conducted by Serge Koussevitzky. 6 sides, 3 12" 78 rpm, with album [1946]. RCA Victor DM-1046.

American Recording Society Orchestra, conducted by Walter Hendl. 1 side, 12" 33 1/3 rpm [1953]. American Recording Society 26.

*Billy the Kid* (Suite from the Ballet)

RCA Victor Symphony Orchestra, conducted by Leonard Bernstein. 1 side, 12" 33 1/3 rpm [1950]. RCA Victor LM-1031. Also 5 sides, 3 7" 45 rpm (RCA Victor WDM-1333) and 5 sides, 3 12" 78 rpm (RCA Victor DM-1333).

*Note: In each of the sets the odd side contains Copland's* Statements: No. 5 (Jingo).

*Prairie Night and Celebration Dance*

New York Philharmonic-Symphony Orchestra, conducted by Leopold Stokowski. 2 sides, 12" 78 rpm [1949]. Columbia 19011-D.

Waltz

Dallas Symphony Orchestra, conducted by Antal Dorati. 1 side, 7" 45 rpm, or 1 side, 12" 78 rpm [1948]. In RCA Victor WDM-1214, or DM-1214 *(Rodeo* album-set).

*The Open Prairie* (arr. piano solo by Lukas Foss)

Oscar Levant, piano. 1 side, 12" 78 rpm [1949]. In Columbia MM-251 (Gershwin Second Rhapsody and Variations on *I Got Rhythm* album-set).

*Celebration Dance, Billy's Demise, The Open Prairie Again*

Whittemore and Lowe, duo-pianists. 1/3 side. 12" 33 1/3 rpm [1952]. RCA Victor LM-1705 *(20th Century Music for Two Pianos).*

Concerto for Clarinet and String Orchestra (with harp and piano)

Benny Goodman, soloist, and Columbia String Orchestra, conducted by Aaron Copland. 1 side, 12" 33 1/3 rpm [1951]. Columbia ML-4421 (with Quartet for Piano and Strings).

Concerto for Piano and Orchestra

Leo Smit, soloist, and Rome Radio Orchestra, conducted by Aaron Copland. 1 side, 12" 33 1/3 rpm [1952]. Concert Hall Society F-4.

*Danzón Cubano*

Leo Smit and Aaron Copland, pianos. 2 sides, 12" 78 rpm [1947]. Concert Hall AL. Also 1/2 side, 10" 33 1/3 rpm [1951]. Concert Hall CHC-51 (with *Three Blues* and *Our Town Suite* [piano solo]).

*El Salón México*

Boston Symphony Orchestra, conducted by Serge Koussevitzky. 3 sides, 2 12" 78 rpm, with album [1939]. RCA Victor DM-546.

*Note: Also released by HMV in England as DB-3812/3.*

Arr. by Johnny Green as *Fantasia Mexicana* for the film, *Fiesta*

Al Goodman's Orchestra. 1 side, 12" 78 rpm [1947]. RCA Victor 28-0419. Also 1 side, 7" 45 rpm [1950?]. RCA Victor 52-0065.

MGM Orchestra, conducted by Macklin Marrow. 2 sides, 10" 78 rpm [1947/8?]. MGM 30016.

Columbia Symphony Orchestra, conducted by Leonard Bernstein. 1 side, 10" 33 1/3 rpm [1951]. Columbia ML-2203.

*Four Piano Blues*

Aaron Copland, piano. 1/2 side, 10" 33 1/3 rpm [1951]. London LPS-298.

*Note: Also released in England on 1 12" 78 rpm disc.*

*Three Blues* (Actually includes two *Blues* and *Sentimental Melody*).

Leo Smit, piano. 1/2 side, 10" 33 1/3 rpm [1951]. Concert Hall CHC-51 (with *Danzón Cubano* [two pianos] and *Our Town Suite* [piano solo]).

*An Immorality*

Vienna State Academy Chamber Chorus, conducted by Ferdinand Grossman. Part of 12" 33 1/3 rpm [1953]. Vox PL-7750 (in Concert of American Music).

*Lincoln Portrait*

Kenneth Spencer, speaker, and New York Philharmonic-Symphony Orchestra, conducted by Artur Rodzinski. 4 sides, 2 12" 78 rpm, with album [1946]. Columbia MX-266. Also 1 side, 10" 33 1/3 rpm [1949]. Columbia ML-2042.

Melvyn Douglas, speaker, and Boston Symphony Orchestra, conducted by Serge Koussevitzky. 3 sides 2 12" 78 rpm, with album [1947]. RCA Victor DM-1088.

*Music for the Theater*

Eastman-Rochester Symphony Orchestra, conducted by Howard Hanson. 6 sides, 3 12" 78 rpm, with album [1941]. RCA Victor DM-744 (withdrawn).

American Recording Society Orchestra, conducted by Walter Hendl. 1 side, 12" 33 1/3 rpm [1952]. American Recording Society 12.

*Old American Songs*

Peter Pears, tenor, and Benjamin Britten, piano. 4 sides, 2 12" 78 rpm [1952]. HMV DA-7038-9.

William Warfield, baritone; Aaron Copland, piano. 1 side, 10" 33 1/3 [1951]. Columbia ML-2206.

Randolph Symonette, bass-baritone. 5/6 side, 12" 33 1/3 rpm [1951]. Colosseum 1008 (in "Americana").

*Our Town* Suite from the Film Score

Leo Smit, piano. 1 side, 10" 33 1/3 rpm [1951]. Concert Hall CHC-51 (with *Three Blues* [piano solo] and *Danzón Cubano* [two pianos]).

*Note: Originally released on 3 sides in a set of 4 12" 78 rpm, with the Piano Sonata, in album-set A2 (limited edition, no longer available).*

Little Orchestra Society, conducted by Thomas Scherman. 1 side, 10" 33 1/3 rpm [1952]. Decca DL-7527.

*Story of Our Town*

Andor Foldes, piano. 1 side, 10" 78 rpm, 16069, in an album-set of 4 10" discs [1947]. Vox 174.

*Note: The collection is entitled* Contemporary American Piano Music, *and also includes short pieces by Barber, Bowles, Harris, Piston, Schuman, Sessions, and Thomson.*

*Outdoor Overture* (arr. for band)

Band of the Irish Guards. 2 sides, 12" 78 rpm. [*c.* 1948]. Boosey and Hawkes 2142.

Piano Sonata

Leonard Bernstein, piano. 5 sides, 3 12" 78 rpm, with album [1949]. RCA Victor DM-1278.

Leo Smit, piano. 5 sides, 3 12" 78 rpm, with album [1946]. Concert Hall A2.

*Note: This set (a limited edition, no longer available) also includes the* Our Town Suite.

Piano Variations

Aaron Copland, piano. 3 sides, 2 12" 78 rpm, with album [1935]. Columbia X-48 (withdrawn).

*Note: The odd side contains the* Nocturne *from Two Pieces for Violin and Piano.*

*Quiet City*

Janssen Symphony of Los Angeles, conducted by Werner Janssen. 1/3 side, 12" 33 1/3 rpm [1950]. Artist 100.

*Note: Included in a set of* Four American Landscapes, *with works by Cowell, Gilbert, and Ives. The set was originally released [1949] on 4 12" 78 rpm discs, with album, as Artist JS-13.*

*Red Pony* Suite from the Film Score

Little Orchestra Society, conducted by Thomas Scherman. 1 side, 12" 33 1/3 rpm [1952]. Decca DL-9616.

*Rodeo: Four Dance Episodes* (from the Ballet)

Dallas Symphony Orchestra, conducted by Antal Dorati. 5 sides, 3 12" 78 rpm, with album [1948]. RCA Victor DM-1214. Also 5 sides, 3 7" 45 rpm, with album [1950] (RCA Victor WDM-1214) and 2 sides, 10" 33 1/3 rpm [1950] (RCA Victor LMX-32).

*Note: In both album-sets the odd side is the Waltz from* Billy the Kid.

Ballet Theatre Orchestra, conducted by Joseph Levine. 1 side, 12" 33 1/3 rpm [1953]. Capitol P-8196.

*Hoe-Down* (arr. for string orchestra)

New Concert String Ensemble, conducted by Jay Wilber. 1 side, 10" 78 rpm [*c.* 1948]. Boosey and Hawkes S-2095.

*Hoe-Down* (arr. for violin and piano)

Louis and Annette Kaufman. 1/7 side, 12" 33 1/3 rpm [1951]. Concert Hall CHC-58.

*Note: In a collection entitled* Americana, *which also includes the* Ukulele Serenade *from Two Pieces for Violin and Piano, and short works by Helm, McBride, Still, and Triggs, and which was released originally [1948] as an album-set of 3 12" 78 rpm discs, Vox 627 (now withdrawn). The LP coupling of* Americana *is* International, *a collection of short works by Achron, Guarnieri, Khachaturian, Milhaud, Prokofieff, and Sibelius.*

*Scherzo Humoristique: The Cat and the Mouse*

Jesús María Sanroma, piano. 1 side, 12" 78 rpm [1940]. RCA Victor 15861 (withdrawn). Included in an album-set, RCA Victor M-646, entitled *Piano Music of the Twentieth Century.*

Sextet

Juilliard String Quartet, with Leonid Hambro, piano, and David Oppenheim, clarinet. 1 side, 12" 33 1/3 rpm [1953]. Columbia ML-4492.

Sonata for Violin and Piano

Joseph Fuchs, violin, and Leo Smit, piano. 1 side, 12" 33 1/3 rpm [1950]. Decca DL-8503.

Fredell Lack, violin, and Leonid Hambro, piano. 1 side, 12" 33 1/3 rpm [1950]. Allegro AL-33.

Louis Kaufman, violin, and Aaron Copland, piano. 5 sides, 3 12" 78 rpm with album [1949]. Concert Hall C-10.

*Note: This set (a limited edition, no longer available) also includes the* Nocturne *from Two Pieces for Violin and Piano.*

*Statements: No. 5 (Jingo)* only

RCA Victor Symphony Orchestra, conducted by Leonard Bernstein. 1 side, 7" 45 rpm, included in an album-set of 3 7" discs [1950]. RCA Victor WDM-1333. Also 1 side, 12" 78 rpm, in RCA Victor album-set DM-1333.

*Note: In both sets the principal work is the* Billy the Kid Suite.

Third Symphony

Minneapolis Symphony Orchestra, conducted by Antal Dorati. Mercury, in preparation.

Two Pieces for String Quartet

Dorian String Quartet. 2 sides, 12" 78 rpm [1940]. Columbia 70092-D (withdrawn).

Two Pieces for Violin and Piano

*Nocturne*

Louis Kaufman, violin, and Aaron Copland, piano. 1 side, 12" 78 rpm, included in an album-set of 3 12" discs (the Violin Sonata) [1949]. Concert Hall C-10 (limited edition, no longer available).

Jacques Gordon, violin, and Aaron Copland, piano. 1 side, 12" 78 rpm, 68321-D, included in an album-set of 2 12" discs (the Piano Variations) [1935]. Columbia X-48 (withdrawn).

*Ukulele Serenade*

Louis and Annette Kaufman. 1/7 side, 12" 33 1/3 rpm [1951]. Concert Hall CHC-58.

*Note: See note under* Rodeo: Hoe-Down.

Jacques Gordon, violin, and Aaron Copland, piano. 1 side, 12" 78 rpm, 68472-D, included in an album-set of 2 12" discs (*Vitebsk*) [1937]. Columbia X-68 (withdrawn).

*Vitebsk* (Trio), Study on a Jewish Theme

Ivor Karman, violin, David Freed, 'cello, and Aaron Copland, piano. 3 sides, 2 12" 78 rpm, with album [1937]. Columbia X-68 (withdrawn).

*Note: The odd side contains the* Ukulele Serenade *from Two Pieces for Violin and Piano.*

Vocalise

Ethel Luening, soprano, and Aaron Copland, piano. 1 side, 12" 78 rpm [1935?]. New Music Quarterly Record 1211 (withdrawn).

Miscellany: *The Music of Aaron Copland for Young People*

New York Philharmonic-Symphony musicians, conducted by Walter Hendl, with Madeleine Lee and Adelaide Klein. 2 sides, 10" 78 rpm [1948]. Young People's Records YPR-408.

*Note: Written by Raymond Abrashkin and including excerpts from* The Red Pony *and other works.*

## III. Articles and Books by Aaron Copland

*Listed in order of publication*

*Gabriel Fauré: A Neglected Master*, in *The Musical Quarterly*, Oct. 1924, pp. 573-86.

*George Antheil*, in *Modern Music*, Jan. 1925, pp. 26-28.

*Letter on Gustav Mahler*, in the New York Times (music page), Apr. 2, 1925.

*America's Young Men of Promise*, in *Modern Music*, Mar.-Apr. 1926, pp. 13-20.

*Playing Safe at Zurich*, in *Modern Music*, Nov.-Dec. 1926, pp. 28-31.

*Jazz Structure and Influence*, in *Modern Music*, Jan.-Feb. 1927, pp. 9-14.

*Baden-Baden, 1927*, in *Modern Music*, Nov.-Dec. 1927, pp. 31-34.

*Stravinsky's "Oedipus Rex"*, in *The New Republic*, Feb. 29, 1928, pp. 68-69.

*Music Since 1920*, in *Modern Music*, Mar.-Apr. 1928, pp. 16-20.

*Carlos Chávez—Mexican Composer*, in *The New Republic*, May 2, 1928, pp. 322-23.

*The Lyricism of Milhaud*, in *Modern Music*, Jan.-Feb. 1929, pp. 14-19.

*From a Composer's Notebook*, in *Modern Music*, May-June 1929, pp. 15-19.

*A Note on Nadia Boulanger*, in *The Fontainebleau Bulletin*, May 1930.

*Modern Orchestration Surveyed by Wellesz*, in *Modern Music*, Nov.-Dec. 1930, pp. 41-44.

*Contemporaries at Oxford, 1931*, in *Modern Music*, Nov.-Dec. 1931, pp. 17-23.

*Stravinsky and Hindemith Premières*, in *Modern Music*, Jan.-Feb. 1932, pp. 85-88.

*The Composer and His Critic*, in *Modern Music*, May-June 1932, pp. 143-47.

*The Composer in America, 1923-1933*, in *Modern Music*, Jan.- Feb. 1933, pp. 87-92.

*One Hundred and Fourteen Songs*, in *Modern Music*, Jan.-Feb. 1934, pp. 59-64.

*Scherchen on Conducting and Ewen on Composers*, in *Modern Music*, Jan.-Feb. 1935, pp. 94-96.

*The American Composer Gets a Break,* in *The American Mercury,* Apr. 1935, pp. 488-92.
*Active Market in New Music Records,* in *Modern Music,* Jan.- Feb. 1936, pp. 45-47.
*Pioneer Listener* [a review of Rosenfeld's *Discoveries of a Music Critic*], in *The New Republic,* Apr. 15, 1936, pp. 291-92.
*Our Younger Generation—Ten Years Later,* in *Modern Music,* May-June 1936, pp. 3-11.
*Mexican Composer—Silvestre Revueltas,* in the New York Times (music page), May 9, 1937.
*What to Listen for in Music.* New York, Whittlesey House, 1939.
*Thomson's Musical State,* in *Modern Music,* Oct-Nov. 1939, pp. 63-65.
*Second Thoughts on Hollywood,* in *Modern Music,* Mar.-Apr. 1940, pp. 141-47.
*The Aims of Music for Films,* in the New York Times (music page), Mar. 10, 1940.
*The Composers Get Wise,* in *Modern Music,* Nov.-Dec. 1940, pp. 18-21.
*The Musical Scene Changes,* in *Twice a Year,* V-VI (1940/41), 340-43.
*Our New Music.* New York, Whittlesey House, 1941.
*Some Notes on My Music for the Theater,* in *The Victor Record Review,* Mar. 1941.
*Five Post-Romantics,* in *Modern Music,* May-June 1941, pp. 218-24. [A chapter from *Our New Music.*]
*The Composers of South America,* in *Modern Music,* Jan.-Feb. 1942, pp. 75-82.
*Latin-Americans in Music,* in *The WQXR Program Book,* June 1942.
*From the '20's to the '40's and Beyond,* in *Modern Music,* Jan.-Feb. 1943, pp. 78-82.
*On the Notation of Rhythm,* in *Modern Music,* May-June 1944, pp. 217-20.
*Serge Koussevitzky and the American Composer,* in *The Musical Quarterly,* July 1944, pp. 255-61.
*The American Composer Today,* in *USA* [government publication], Vol. 2, No. 10 [n. d.], pp. 23-27.
*Fauré Festival at Harvard,* in the New York Times (music page), Nov. 25, 1945.
*Neglected Works: A Symposium,* in *Modern Music,* Winter 1946, pp. 7-8.
*Memorial to Paul Rosenfeld,* in *Notes,* Mar. 1947, pp. 147-48.
*South American Report,* in the New York Times (music page), Dec. 21, 1947.
*The New "School" of American Composers,* in the New York Times (magazine section), Mar. 14, 1948.
*First Symphony by Darius Milhaud* [record review], in *The Saturday Review of Literature,* June 26, 1948, p. 43.

*Stefan Wolpe: Two Songs* [music review], in *Notes,* Dec. 1948, p. 172.

*Influence, Problem, Tone* [tribute to Stravinsky], in Minna Lederman, ed., *Stravinsky in the Theatre,* New York, 1949, pp. 121-22.

*The Personality of Stravinsky,* in Edwin Corle, ed., *Igor Stravinsky,* New York, 1949, pp. 121-22.

*The Music of Israel by Peter Gradenwitz* [book review], in the New York Herald Tribune (book section), Oct. 2, 1949.

*Tip to Moviegoers: Take Off Those Ear-Muffs,* in the New York Times (magazine section), Nov. 6, 1949.

*The World of A-Tonality* [review of *Schoenberg and His School* by René Leibowitz], in the New York Times (book section), Nov. 27, 1949.

*Contemporary Music—Is it Peculiar?,* in the New York Times (magazine section), Dec. 15, 1949.

*Duo for violin and piano by Leon Kirchner* (music review), in *Notes,* June, 1950.

*The American Musical Scene,* in *Musik Olympiad,* Salzburg, Vol. 1, No. 1.

*Fourth String Quartet by William Schuman* (music review), in *Musical Quarterly,* July, 1951.

*Music and Imagination,* Cambridge, Mass., Harvard University Press, 1952.

*An Indictment of the Fourth B,* in the New York Times (magazine section), Sept. 21, 1952.

*Creativity in America,* in Proceedings, National Institute of Arts and Letters, 1953.

*Notes Without Music by Darius Milhaud* (book review), in the New York Times (book section) Feb. 22, 1953.

## IV. Selected Bibliography of Articles on and References to Aaron Copland

*The entries are arranged alphabetically by author*

Antheil, George. *American Music Must Grow Up,* in *Tomorrow,* Feb. 1949, pp. 34 f.

Bauer, Marion. *Copland,* in David Ewen, ed., *The Book of Modern Composers,* New York, 2nd ed., 1950, pp. 471-78.

——— *Aaron Copland,* in Elie Siegmeister, ed., *The Music Lover's Handbook,* New York, 1943, pp. 757-61.

Berger, Arthur. *The Piano Variations of Aaron Copland,* in *The Musical Mercury,* Aug.-Sept. 1934, pp. 85-86.

——— *Music Chronicle: Copland's Piano Sonata,* in *Partisan Review,* Mar.-Apr. 1943, pp. 187-90.

——— *Aspects of Aaron Copland's Music,* in *Tempo,* Mar. 1945, pp. 2-5.

——— *The Music of Aaron Copland,* in *The Musical Quarterly,* Oct. 1945, pp. 420-47.

——— *The Third Symphony of Aaron Copland,* in *Tempo,* Autumn 1948, pp. 20-27.

——— *The Home-Grown Copland,* in *The Staurday Review of Literature,* Nov. 25, 1950, pp. 72, 76.

——— *Aaron Copland,* in *Perspectives USA,* Fall 1952, pp. 105-130.

Brook, Donald. *Composers Gallery,* London, 1946, pp. 133-36.

Chanler, Theodore. *Aaron Copland,* in Henry Cowell, ed., *American Composers on American Music,* Stanford, 1933, pp. 49-56.

Citkowitz, Israel. *Personal Note,* in David Ewen, ed., *The Book of Modern Composers,* New York, 2nd ed., 1950, pp. 465-67.

Diamond, David. *The Composer and Film Music,* in *Decision,* Mar. 1941, pp. 57-60.

Eyer, Ronald F. *Meet the Composer: Aaron Copland,* in *Musical America,* Dec. 10, 1943, pp. 7, 27.

Flanagan, William. *American Songs,* in *Musical America,* Feb. 1952, p. 23.

Fuller, Donald. *A Symphonist Goes to Folk Sources,* in *Musical America,* Feb. 1948, pp. 29, 256, 397.

Goldberg, Isaac. *Aaron Copland and his Jazz,* in *The American Mercury,* Sept. 1927, pp. 63-65.

Heinsheimer, Hans W. *Aaron Copland: The Making of an American Composer,* in *Tomorrow,* Nov. 1947, pp. 17-21.

Krenek, Ernst. *Musik im Goldenen Westen,* Vienna, 1949, pp. 15, 28, 38, 62.

Kubly, Herbert. *America's No. 1 Composer,* in *Esquire,* Apr. 1948, pp. 57, 143-45.

Lederman, Minna. *Some American Composers,* in *Vogue,* Feb. 1, 1947, p. 231.

Mellers, W. H. *American Music (An English Perspective),* in *Kenyon Review,* Summer 1943, pp. 370-75.

——— *Music and Society,* London, 1946, pp. 139-41.

——— *Aaron Copland and the American Idiom,* in *Tempo,* Autumn 1948, pp. 17-20.

Moor, Paul. *Aaron Copland,* in *Theatre Arts,* Jan. 1951, pp. 40-45.

Morton, Lawrence. *About Aaron,* in *Script,* June 15, 1940, pp. 18-19.

——— *Music Notes,* in *Script,* Mar. 20, 1943, p. 24.

——— *The Red Pony,* in *Film Music Notes* (Special Issue), Feb. 1949.
Rosenfeld, Paul. *By Way of Art,* New York, 1928, pp. 266-72.
——— *An Hour with American Music,* Philadelphia, 1929, pp. 126-43.
——— *Discoveries of a Music Critic,* New York, 1936, pp. 332-37.
——— *The Advance of American Music,* in *Kenyon Review,* Spring 1939, pp. 185-90.
——— *Current Chronicle,* in *The Musical Quarterly,* July 1939, pp. 372-76.
Salas, Juan Orrego. *Aaron Copland: A New York Composer,* in *Tempo,* Autumn 1948, pp. 8-16.
Salazar, Adolfo. *Music in Our Time,* New York, 1946, pp. 328-31.
Saminsky, Lazare. *Living Music of the Americas,* New York, 1949, pp. 127-32.
Sargeant, Winthrop. *The Case of Aaron Copland,* in *Tomorrow,* June 1946, pp. 54-56.
Sternfeld, Frederick. *Copland as Film Composer,* in *Musical Quarterly,* April 1951, pp. 161-175.
Thompson, Oscar. *Aaron Copland,* in Oscar Thompson, ed., *Great Modern Composers,* Cleveland, 1943, pp. 41-48.
Thomson, Virgil. *Aaron Copland,* in *Modern Music,* Jan.-Feb. 1932, pp. 67-73.

# Index